RAISING A CREATIVE CHILD

CHALLENGING ACTIVITIES AND GAMES FOR YOUNG MINDS

Cynthia MacGregor

A Citadel Press Book
Published by Carol Publishing Group

A Citadel Press Book
Published by Carol Publishing Group
Citadel Press is a registered trademark of Carol Communications, Inc.
Editorial Offices: 600 Madison Avenue, New York, N.Y. 10022
Sale and Distribution Offices: 120 Enterprise Avenue, Secaucus, N.J. 07094
In Canada: Canadian Manda Group, One Atlantic Avenue, Suite 105, Toronto, Ontario M6K 3E7
Queries regarding rights and permissions should be addressed to Carol Publishing Group, 600 Madison Avenue, New York, N.Y. 10022

Carol Publishing Group books are available at special discounts for bulk purchases, sales promotion, fund-raising, or educational purposes. Special editions can be created to specifications. For details, contact: Special Sales Department, Carol Publishing Group, 120 Enterprise Avenue, Secaucus, N.J. 07094

Manufactured in the United States of America
10 9 8 7 6 5 4 3 2 1

Library of Congress Cataloging-in-Publication Data

MacGregor, Cynthia.
    Raising a creative child : challenging activities and games for young minds / Cynthia MacGregor.
        p.   cm.
    "A Citadel Press book."
    ISBN 0-8065-1741-7 (pbk.)
    1. Child development—Miscellanea.   2. Child rearing—Miscellanea.
    3. Creative activities and seatwork.   I. Title.
    HQ767.9.M27   1996
    305.23'1—dc20   95-47102
                                                        CIP

RAISING A CREATIVE CHILD

Also by Cynthia MacGregor

Why Do We Need Another Baby?
Moon Love
Family Customs and Traditions
Mommy, I'm Bored
Creative Family Projects, Games, and Activities
An Appetite for Passion
One Heart's Opinion
Totally Terrific Family Games
Free Family Fun
Mommy, There's Nothing To Do

For David
With love

And for Laurel
With love
And with the hope she'll use this book well

Contents

Acknowledgments

As always, my heartfelt thanks to Vic Bobb for his invaluable assistance.

Thanks this time, too, to Lenna Buissink.

Introduction

"But I picture my child becoming a lawyer, not an artist."

And so you don't think your child needs to be creative? Think again. Creativity is as necessary to the man or woman who wields control in the courtroom or the boardroom as it is to the one who wields a paintbrush. Creativity yields solutions to business problems as well as it serves up sunsets on canvas—or symphonies, poetry, or other forms of artistic expression. Creativity serves each and every one of us, each and every day.

If you're in the kitchen dreaming up a new recipe, finding a way to improve on an old one, or even arranging dinner attractively on a serving platter, you're being creative.

If you're unsuccessfully trying to balance your checkbook and come up with a solution to find your error, you're being creative.

If you're a doctor who thinks of a novel solution for a patient in distress, a lawyer who comes up with a brilliant argument before a jury, or a plumber who reroutes pipes in a way that solves a problem, you're being creative.

If you're a parent who thinks of a new way to reward or discipline your child, to get your kids to do their homework, or to resolve sibling warfare, you're being creative.

Creativity can even help you think of an occupation to get into, as well as help you once you settle into it. I recently met a woman who decided that with her flair for organization she could help people organize their homes, offices, and closets. She now makes a living doing just that—and charges $35 an hour to the people she helps. Creativity abounds in all areas of life.

Creativity is an everyday necessity. And some of us possess more of it than others do. True, some of us are just born more creative than others. But creativity can be developed—or stifled. The parent who says, "Sunsets aren't green, you're painting that wrong" is stifling a creative child's explorations. On the other hand, there are things you can do to encourage and develop your child's creativity.

Like the actual muscles in a person's body, the creativity "muscles" need to be stretched and exercised, too. But while physical workouts are truly that—work, and hard work at that—exercising the creativity muscles can be just plain fun.

Some of the exercises in this book are games you can play with your child, or games she can play by herself or with other kids. Pure fun, but your child will develop those creative muscles while she's enjoying the activities. Others are questions to pose to your child, questions designed to stretch those muscles by provoking thought or imagination. Still others are different types of activities, but all are aimed at helping your child grow in creativity.

Whatever your aspirations for your child, he'll be served better—in his professional and personal life—if he's a creative thinker, a creative person. So start stretching those muscles now!

RAISING A CREATIVE CHILD

Chapter 1

Write On!

The ability to write is important even for a child who has no aspirations to be a novelist, playwright, journalist, poet, or lyricist. Just being able to express himself clearly in a business letter is important. And suppose he has to give a speech some day. Will he be able to express his thoughts well? There are many situations in which being able to write well is important, and the person who can write well can usually use the spoken word more clearly, too. Good communication is vital.

The activities in this section are designed to give your child practice in different kinds of writing, and hopefully make him or her better at it, too. As with all the activities in the book, some are going to be more appealing to your child than others. If she loves writing but has no interest in poetry, it's good to encourage her to try her hand at poetry, but if she balks insistently, or hates poetry outright, don't force the issue. You don't want her to wind up hating writing altogether because she was required to write poems.

Greetings!

Christmas cards, birthday cards, Mother's Day and Father's Day cards—there's no end to the occasions for which greeting cards are available. And now there's a trend toward people sending greeting cards just for fun, or to say "I'm thinking about you," "I love you," "I miss you," or "You're my friend."

Ask your child to design and create greeting cards out of construction paper, typing paper, or any other suitable paper you have in the house. If he doesn't want to actually draw the art and create the whole card, at least have him write the sentiments for the fronts and insides of the cards.

Besides the usual occasions, suggest your child create cards for the following:

- new pet
- lost pet
- new brother or sister
- elementary school graduation
- straight-A report card
- winning an honor in school

What other occasions can your child think of to create cards for?

Good Fortune to You

A close second to the meal itself, the fortune cookies in Chinese restaurants are an enjoyable treat for most kids. But your child doesn't have to wait till you next have Chinese food to enjoy the fun of printed fortunes. In fact, she can have a turn at writing the fortunes herself.

Your child can write a number of fortunes compactly on a sheet of paper, printing neatly and as small as she can. The fortunes can be the predictive variety ("You will marry someone rich and have seven kids."), the advice variety ("The more you keep your mouth shut, the less you need to worry about putting your foot in it."), or some of each.

When the fortunes have all been written, your child can cut each one out of the sheet of paper, and they are ready to be distributed. If she has one or more siblings, she can have the fun of distributing the fortunes as well as writing them. If two or more siblings worked on the fortunes together, you can pool them for distribution so nobody knows which one she's getting, or even whether it's one she wrote herself or one created by a sibling.

If your child is an "only," you may want to hand the fortunes out to her at your discretion. Even though she knows what they say, she doesn't know which one she'll get or where one is going to pop up.

Where's a good place to tuck away a fortune?

- in your child's lunchbox
- folded into everyone's napkins at the dinner table
- rolled up in socks
- folded into t-shirts
- in her school book bag or pencil case
- tucked among the clothes in your child's trunk when she goes off to summer camp
- between the pages of an encyclopedia or dictionary—the fortune applies to whoever first turns to that page and finds it
- Anywhere else you and your child can think of as suitable

Happily Ever After... and Then What?

Supposedly Cinderella lived happily ever after—but was the road totally smooth? Or did she encounter bumps in the road of life?

Surely Cinderella had some further adventures after her prince found that her shoe fit. For one thing, she and Prince

Charming probably had children. How many? Were they boys or girls? What were their names? What were they like? Does a princess face situations with her kids that are similar to those faced by the moms your child knows? Or is palace life substantially different for moms and kids?

Take Snow White and the seven dwarfs. What did the dwarfs do after Snow White went off with her prince? Did they meet another young woman in the forest? Did they build their mining venture into a big business? And what of Snow White and *her* prince? Like Cinderella and Prince Charming, did they have kids? What were *their* names?

Practical Pig's brick house kept the wolf on the other side of the door—till the fire in the chimney did him in. What did the three pigs do afterward? Did the other two pigs finally learn their lesson? Or did they go back to their lazy, procrastinating ways? Meanwhile, did the big bad wolf have a cousin with a similar yen for pork?

Suggest that your child write the "story after the story" for those mentioned above, or Peter Pan, Hansel and Gretel, Rapunzel, or any other story he knows well.

His Name Is His Story

A fun activity that challenges kids' creativity is writing a very short story in as many words as there are letters in the child's name. Each sentence will begin with one letter of your child's name, in order. Lost? I'll unconfuse you.

Say your son's name is Tommy. The first sentence of his story is going to start with a *T*, the second with an *O*, the third with an *M*, the fourth with another *M*, and the last with a *Y*. Let's look at a sample written according to these rules:

Today I saw a boy crying in the schoolyard. "Oh, you look sad, I said." "My lunch money's gone," he said. "Maybe I could share my lunch with you," I offered. "Yes, thank you!" he answered gratefully.

Your child can even use his full name instead of nickname. Tommy might decide the letters T–H–O–M–A–S offer more storyline possibilities than the letters T–O–M–M–Y.

Here's another story, as it might be written by a girl named Amelia:

A Martian landed on Earth. Martians had never been to Earth before. Earth is very different from Mars. Looking around, she decided this wouldn't be a bad planet to settle down on. Immediately she sent a message to her home planet, saying that her fellow Martians should follow here. All the inhabitants of Mars will be here next Tuesday.

And Now a Word From Our Sponsor

This activity has a double benefit: Not only does your child have fun while getting in some writing practice, he also gets to think about how advertisements can manipulate people.

First, ask your child to study the commercials he sees every day on TV. He probably knows the name of every product regularly advertised on the shows he watches, but he should pay attention not to the product but to how it's being sold—what techniques are being used to make it seem attractive, to make the viewer want the product, and to impel the viewer to go out and buy it. (Once your child realizes how he's being manipulated, his natural contrariness may set in and he may be a little less willing to let himself be swayed by advertisements.)

You can also point out some printed advertisements to your child. He's been exposed to these before, too, though probably not as relentlessly as the broadcast ads. Still, if he reads the newspaper to cut out current event items for school, subscribes to a magazine that has ads, has ever flipped through some of your magazines to find pictures to cut out, or peruses *TV Guide,* or your local paper's TV magazine, he's run into a fair share of print ads. And if he listens to the radio—which he almost certainly does—he's heard plenty of commercials there too. Again, he should now listen to a few of them with a different ear, listening for the ways that advertisers make their pitch, making their product seem like a must-have.

You might even want to discuss with your child the various techniques used to make consumers buy products. Whatever your child's age, he can probably understand the following simple concepts:

• Some ads try to convince you that Brand X is better than Brand Y so you'll buy Brand X cereal, candy, or building blocks instead of the competition.

• Some ads try to convince you that a product is something you have to have. In these cases, the question isn't so much whether you're going to buy Brand X or Brand Y, but whether you're going to buy that product at all. The company wants you to buy their product rather than save your money.

• Some ads appeal just to your emotions. They don't attempt to convince you with logic that you should buy their product. Rather, they use music, words, and pictures that give you a good feeling, and then they mention their product. They want you to keep that good feeling inside while you think about their product so, feeling good about it, you'll buy it.

Most kids can understand these concepts, or some variation of them. You can even watch commercials or read print ads with your child, asking, "Now, in what way is the advertiser trying to get you to buy their product?"

Now that your child has a rudimentary comprehension of how Madison Avenue works, it's time for him to write some commercials himself. You can ask him to write an assortment of different types. For starters, choose from this list:

• Commercials for existing products. These could be cereals, toys, or some other product that your child uses. It could be a product that he has seen around the house or one whose name he is familiar with from seeing real commercials for it on TV.

• Commercials for made-up products. Here he can *really* let his imagination run wild, dreaming up the product, its name and slogan, as well as one or more ads for it. What products will your child dream up? Will they be logical, practical, fanciful, extravagantly impossible? Will he come up with a nonexistent brand of a real product (Puppy Love Dog Food, Glisten Shampoo) or a product that doesn't even exist in real life (Fresh bottled rainwater, E-Z-Carry book bag on wheels)? It may even be a fanciful product of his wishful thinking (Edu-Robbie, the robot that does your homework, Insta-Clean, the machine that straightens your room).

• Commercials for himself or a friend for class president, student council president, safety monitor, or some other elected office.

• Commercials for real politicians running for elected office. (If he doesn't know who some of our elected officials are and is old enough to, now would be a good time to launch that discussion.)

• Commercials that make unappetizing real-life products or situations seem more appealing. For example: a commercial giving good reasons to do your homework or to do it promptly; a commercial for spinach (or whatever veggie your child hates most); a commercial exhorting kids on the value of being in the class of the strictest teacher in the school.

• Public service announcements. Suitable themes include Don't Start Smoking, Keep Off Drugs, and Buckle Up, though your child can feel free to write any other public service announcements he thinks of, including those aimed at adults as well as kids. (These might include Don't Drink and Drive, Don't Speed, Give Blood Regularly, and Register and Vote.)

The Play's the Thing

Play. To most kids, that's a verb describing their favorite activity. But it's also a noun describing a dramatized story. Why doesn't your child try his hand at writing one?

Stretching the creativity muscles means more than just exercising them. It means making them grow—and in new directions. Your child has probably written stories, but has he ever tried his hand at writing a play?

Don't worry about stage directions and such—all that's needed here is dialogue, except where an action is crucial to the story. And for a first-time playwright, total originality isn't even needed. Your child can write a dramatized version of any existing story. It will be a better exercise if he chooses one that doesn't already exist as a movie. It could be a dramatization of Rapunzel, or a play about the Three Billy Goats Gruff, or any other story your child is familiar with.

If your child is at all interested in acting, have him gather a group of friends to put on a performance of the script he's written. The audience can be family, friends, or neighborhood kids. But even if, the play is never performed, he will still be proud of his script.

If he is at all successful in dramatizing a familiar story, suggest that he next write a totally original play. It can be about familiar characters (like "The Further Adventures of Cinderella") or completely original.

A Play With No Actors

Another kind of play your child can write is a puppet show. Again, this can be totally original, an original play based on familiar characters, or a dramatization of a familiar story. If your child already has puppets, great; if not, you can buy a few inexpensive ones, or she can make them out of thread spools or socks. To make a rudimentary sock puppet, stuff about half the foot of a pale (white, beige, light tan) sock. Cotton works best for the stuffing, but foam rubber will work too. Either paint the face on or sew two buttons on for eyes and another for a nose, and possibly glue on crepe paper for eyebrows as well as a mouth. The child can embellish the features with crepe paper hair (or cotton for white hair) and add any additional improvements she wishes, such as a row of three buttons running down the front from a point a couple of inches below the puppet's mouth to suggest clothes.

To make a rudimentary spool puppet, just paint a face on an empty thread spool and use crepe paper, cotton, or other suitable material for hair. Break off the point of a sharpened pencil and glue the pencil into the bottom end of the spool. Then hold the bottom of the pencil to maneuver the puppet.

If you don't have a fancy puppet theater and no one in the family is a carpenter, you can open a card table, lay it on its side, and have the child get behind the table to present the puppet show. Or drape a tablecloth over the dining room table so it hangs all the way down to the floor on one side. Then have the child get on the far side. Protected from the audience's view by the tablecloth, she can manipulate the puppets above the top of the table. On with the show!

Homemade Dictionary

Some families have words of their own, words that every member of that family knows. (See the book *Family Words,* by Paul Dickson.) And many kids make up words whose definitions are known only to them, or perhaps their friends. Adults get into the act too, sometimes without kids being involved. (See the book *Sniglets,* by Rich Hall.)

Your child can create his own words, and even make a dictionary out of them if he devises enough words to fill a small homemade book. But let's not put the cart before the horse—first he needs to dream up the words and their definitions.

Sometimes words just naturally sound like the thing they describe; others bear no discernible relationship to their meanings but just sound right to the person who coins them. Some are combinations of existing English words, which when used together have a new meaning. If Dad frequently taps his foot impatiently—and loudly—on the floor when annoyed, Evan might say to his sister Kayla, "Now's not a good time to ask Dad for that raise in your allowance—it's foot music time." "Foot music time" would be a perfectly understandable term to Kayla even if she'd never heard the phrase before. A new expression is born—and one for Evan's dictionary.

The dictionary itself is not the important part of this activity—it's dreaming up the words and their meanings that is most important. But your child may want to keep his list of new words in a form more formal than just a list, mental or written.

In that case, he can make a dictionary using sheets of construction paper or typing paper stapled together between construction paper covers. On these sheets he can write each word and its definition in alphabetical order. Instead of stapling the pages, he can use a separate page for each word and bind the pages with a fastener, or hole-punch them and collect them in a loose-leaf binder. In this way he can add more words and expressions as he thinks of them without having to rewrite the whole book.

Since dictionaries frequently illustrate some of their entries, if your child likes to draw he can provide pictures to accompany some of the words he includes.

A Letter Across the Ocean

No matter what your ethnicity, your child's ancestors originally came from somewhere else. Even Native Americans' ancestors originally crossed a land bridge that no longer exists but once carried them here from another continent.

If your child doesn't have a good grounding in her ancestors' origins, now would be a good time to explain where Great-Grandpa or Great-Great-Grandma came from and, if you know, *why* each ancestor emigrated. Also, if your child is not familiar with the country and time of each ancestor's origin—eighteenth century Germany, Cuba in the 1940s, Wales in the 1850s, or colonial Australia—now's a good time to give her a little background.

In this activity, your child should write an imaginary letter from her ancestor to a friend left behind. In it, this ancestor might write of:

- the conditions he found on arriving here
- how things differed from the land he left behind
- what his aspirations are for himself and his family, as well as future generations
- what it's like to be an outsider in a new land (perhaps where a different language is spoken if the ancestor emigrated from a non-English-speaking country,

She might also speak of:

- where he is living (the city, town, or state, whether it's an urban or rural area, whether he lives in a house, apartment, or shack)
- whom he's living with (other family members, strangers, friends, or alone)
- Whether this new land is at all like what he expected

If you and your child don't know exactly when this ancestor

arrived or precisely where he came from, creative latitude is permitted. If you don't know the exact reasons for the emigration—poor finances in the old country and greater opportunity here, political oppression in the old country and the promise of freedom here, capture and enslavement in Africa, or following another family member who came over earlier —making up details is not only permitted but encouraged.

If this ancestor was not literate, this should not prevent the child from writing the letter anyway. After all, this is an exercise in imagination. If she wishes, your child can pretend the letter was dictated by her ancestor to a friend who could write.

If she enjoys the activity, try it again another day, with a different ancestor. After all, even if you and your spouse were recent immigrants yourselves, that gives your child two people's parts to play. If your parents were immigrants, that gives your child four people to write letters to, and if your parents' grandparents were the immigrants, your child has sixteen personae to assume at different times.

Westward, Ho!

In a vein similar to the activity above, ask your child to pretend he's a pioneer in the great westward migration. In fact, one of your child's ancestors may well have been among the riders of the westbound wagons. This may even have been one of the same ancestors whose personae your child assumed in "A Letter Across the Ocean." But for this activity, it doesn't matter if your child's ancestors migrated westward or if the entire family has hugged the Eastern Seaboard ever since arriving on these shores. Your child needs only to pretend he's a pioneer, regardless of your family's true history.

There are three activities your child can engage in as a pretend pioneer, all of which call for writing.

1) **Hello From the Prairies.** In this activity, your child should

imagine what life was like for a child migrating west, as part of a wagon train or otherwise, and write a letter back home to a friend on the East Coast.

The letter might tell of the experience of moving, traveling across the immensity of the plains, leaving all familiar things behind, facing the unknown, having dangerous adventures, and anticipating and speculating about the "new world" waiting at the end of the Oregon Trail, or whatever route they're taking.

2) **A Pioneer Child's Diary.** Having arrived at the western end of the journey, the family would now settle in to their new life. If the pioneer child kept a diary, it might tell of:

- arriving at their destination
- what sort of landscape was waiting for them
- what conditions were like
- what kind of structure they built to live in
- whether a town already existed there or nearby
- where they got food
- what the nearest neighbors were like
- the sort of clothes the family now wore and how these compared with the clothes they'd worn back East
- the games they played
- what sort of schooling they received
- any other details the child felt like providing

Your child can write such a diary. If he's unsure of some of the details that would give it the ring of authenticity, you can guide him to the library, and books that tell of the life of pioneers, especially young pioneers. Even if he knows all the answers, writing this diary may create a hunger in him to learn more about those westward pioneer days.

3) **I Remember the Old Days.** This one *really* calls for stretching the imagination. Your child is asked to pretend that he's a former pioneer who has lived to today as a very old but still mentally alert person. Looking back on the old days, he

compares them to modern times and tells what's better about current ones, and in what way the old days were better.

He can compare those times with these in general, or talk about being a child today. Games, schooling, entertainment, living conditions, family togetherness, or any other aspect of life—all are suitable for discussion.

Pretending to be a *very* old person who was a child during the westward migration and lived to see the modern era—that requires quite a stretch of the imagination!

A Letter of Historical Importance

I need to preface this activity by warning that, of all those in this book, this may be the one that seems most like homework and least like fun. If your child is a history buff, she may love it; ditto if she's already an avowed future writer. Otherwise you may meet with some resistance when suggesting this activity. But it's at least worth trying, so suggest your child try her hand at it, as this activity will not only exercise her creative muscles but increase her knowledge of history at the same time.

Ask your child to pretend she's present at any event of historical significance and write a letter home about it. Let *her* choose the event to be described. By giving her that choice, you increase her interest in the activity.

It's optional whether she pretends to be the person most instrumental in the incident, another participant, or an onlooker. She can choose to "be" Dolley Madison helping evacuate the White House before the British set fire to it, a White House staffer who was present and can report on the event, or a Washington resident who watched from the street.

She can be Leif Erikson landing on the North American continent, or one of his crew; the pilot of the Enola Gay; Columbus, one of his crew, or a Native American watching the ships sail toward shore. She can tell about discovering the process of vulcanizing rubber or pasteurizing milk, about discovering penicillin or electricity. Maybe she was flying a kite alongside Ben Franklin in that thunderstorm.

Whatever incident she chooses to describe, she's going to write about it in a letter to family members who weren't present while history was being made. In this letter she'll describe the trek through the Dust Bowl; the optimism, successes, disappointments, and hardships of the California gold strike; or whatever historical time or moment she's chosen.

If your child really gets into this but is not familiar with the event in question, she may even wind up researching it and improving her research skills along with her creativity.

Plot-in-a-Pot

Sometimes creativity needs a little nudge. For instance, there are kids who are perfectly capable of writing a story but need a "jump start" to get going. Even professional writers sometimes need a little help. Long before plot-generating software was available to today's computer-based writers, a set of cards with plots on them was making its way around writing circles in the 1930s.

Plot-in-a-Pot works on the same principle as aids for professional writers: The child who encounters writer's block can still write a story if handed the framework on which to construct it. Give him a plot and characters, and the rest will follow. Though the spark comes from the outside, the child is still being truly creative; even though the framework has been provided for him, what he builds on that framework is all his own.

Plot-in-a-Pot can be adapted to various age levels and levels of writing ability. Let's talk here about a child of ten or older, one who already knows it's fun to make up stories. If your child is younger or has little or no experience in writing fiction, you'll want to make some adjustments to the suggestions that follow.

In preparing Plot-in-a-Pot for your child, you'll need the following materials: several containers (the "pots"—which can literally be pots, bowls, or other containers), slips of paper or index cards, and a pen or pencil.

At a minimum, you need two containers. One should be labelled "Characters," and the other "Plot Problems." Additionally, you may wish to add one for "Characteristics," another for "Settings," and another for "Complications."

It's up to you to write an assortment of items for each container. Each time your child engages in this activity, he picks one item from each of the containers, with the exception of "Characters," from which he may choose to pick more than one.

If you've only provided characters and plot problems, he writes a story about the character he pulled from the characters container, with the problem he has pulled from the plot problems container, devising the rest of the story himself.

If you have provided containers for all the categories, your child will have many of the elements of the story already in place after dipping once into each container. But he will still have only a framework and has plenty of creating to do.

You need to make sure the items on the slips are ones the child can relate to, either from his own life, that part of your life that he's familiar with, books he's read, or movies he's seen. The child with a parent who works in a factory will probably know what a quality control inspector is if he encounters this person on character slip. The child whose parents are shoe store clerks, lawyers, agricultural workers, or teachers may not have the foggiest clue what you're talking about.

Almost any child will be able to relate to "teacher," "grandmother," "police officer," and other such familiar types.

But stretch your child's boundaries. Include characters and settings that are outside the list of people he encounters every day, as long as they're not references so obscure that he draws a complete blank on seeing the words. Assuming he has some idea of what these people do, include "harvest truck driver," "ironworker," or "newscaster," along with "pilot," "mail carrier," or whatever more familiar poeple you put in the characters container.

In the characteristics container, if you have one, you can put single adjectives or longer descriptions: "angry," "worried," "sneaky," "dishonest," "kind," "caring," "unemployed," "interfering," "optimistic," or "eager for the start of school," "concerned about money," "afraid of losing his or her job," "filled with Christmas spirit."

In the plot problems container, you can put generalized plot problems ("struggle to perform a duty," "solve a mystery") or more specific problems ("learn to do twenty pushups by the beginning of team tryouts," "earn enough money to buy Mother a really special Christmas present," "find out who stole Lisa's bracelet," "find out whom the dog he found belongs to," or "convince Mom to let him keep the dog he found").

The settings container, as with the characters container, should contain references to places familiar to the child. This does not mean the child has to have visited the site personally. If she's read *Heidi,* you could probably include "the Swiss Alps" on one slip of paper. Settings can be generic or specific. "A house at the shore" is fine, as is "a circus tent," "a school," or "a high mountain." It doesn't have to be a particular place, such as Three Rivers Stadium or Madison Square Garden, but it certainly can be. It can also be a fictitious setting.

The complications container contains such plot-complicating situations as "a fire," "an illness," "a robbery," "no money," or "loses his or her job."

The child will draw at least one slip from the characters

container; he can draw more than one if he wants to have two protagonists, a protagonist and an antagonist, or simply a secondary character for the main character to interact with.

Let's stretch our own imaginations for the moment, and imagine that your child draws "teacher" from characters, "tired" from characteristics, "out at the lake" from settings, "struggle to perform a duty" from plot problems, and "fire" from complications.

Now he has to write a story about a tired teacher out at a lake who struggles to perform a duty but is somehow thwarted by a fire. As you can see, though you've given your child the bare-bones essentials, he still has to write a whole story, or tell one aloud if you make this an oral activity.

All sorts of details are needed. We certainly need to know something more about the teacher than just that he's tired. *Why* is he tired? What's he doing at the lake? What is the duty or obligation he needs to meet, and why is it important? What about this fire? How is it going to start, and how will it be put out? And how will the teacher overcome this adversity to triumph in the end? Or will he? Not all stories have happy endings!

If your child gets a lot of use and enjoyment out of Plot-in-a-Pot, you can rotate the elements in the containers. Of course, if he's picked "school principal," "grumpy," "haunted house," "save a life," and "heavy snow" as the elements of one story, you can return those to their respective containers. Even if your child picks "school principal" again tomorrow, you know it's highly unlikely he'll pick any of the other same elements along with it. A story about an overzealous school principal in a firehouse, who has to make a critical decision, with the complication of the illness of a best friend, is going to be a very different story, despite the fact that the protagonist is in the same profession as the protagonist of the last story.

If you want, you can "retire" used story elements temporarily to another container, replace them with fresh elements, or if the container was initially well-stocked, simply let your child work from a diminished reservoir. After a respectable interval, bring the used elements out of retirement and return them to the appropriate containers. If your child gets a lot of use out of Plot-in-a-Pot, you'll want to expand the contents of the containers regularly.

Plot-in-a-Pot isn't just about jump-starting kids who want to write stories but can't quite get going. It will also help them to understand the construction of a story—interesting characters, a goal to be met or a problem to be solved, an obstacle or conflict that gets in the way of achieving that goal, and a resolution to the conflict and the story. It will also help them better understand the construction of books and stories they read and perhaps be more discerning readers who understand *why* a particular book or story works—or doesn't.

Plot-in-a-Pot also works as a car game for keeping a child occupied on long trips, as the contents of the containers can easily be transferred into small plastic bags for easy portability. And two or more children can engage in Plot-in-a-Pot, telling their stories aloud rather than writing them. It's a good noncompetitive activity, as well as being creativity-stretching.

Treasure Seekers

Sherlock Holmes wasn't the only one who loved a mystery. Kids love mysteries too, and secrets, and in this game there's plenty of both that will not only exercise your child's creativity but her ingenuity as well.

For the first round of the game, you hide the treasure and write the clues. The treasure can be a small toy, a piece of cake or candy, a quarter, or anything else that your child will be pleased to find but isn't extravagant. The clues will lead her to the treasure, step by step.

The first clue, which you should hand to your child, should be written in a somewhat mysterious manner. If you'd like, it can also be in rhyme. When deciphered, it's a clue to the location of the next one. When your child deciphers the first clue and locates the second, she'll find that it, too, is written somewhat mysteriously and leads to the location of the third clue. On and on it goes, perhaps through four clues, perhaps through twelve. The number is limited only by the amount of patience your child has, the number of hiding places in your home, and your ability to write good mysterious clues. The final clue leads the child to the hiding place of the treasure.

Once your child understands how the game is played and how the clues are written, it's her turn to hide the treasure, write the clues, and offer a treasure hunt to a friend, brother, sister, or neighbor. The clues can be brief but mysterious, labyrinthian, or poetic. Just how mysterious you can get will depend on your child's age and ability to unravel the mystery. Examples of possible clues follow:

You'll have to get Monica out of the way
If you wish to find this clue today.
If you find your sister, the clue's not far.
It's where girls her age always are.

The next clue is somewhere around the phone.

Things are really heating up down under, and I don't mean in Australia.

The next clue is tucked in the range hood—the stove and oven being "down under" it.

Noah's Ark wasn't the only site for two-by-two arrangements.

The next clue is tucked in your child's sock drawer.

You'll have to go to Africa on your hunt for the next clue.

It's between pages of the encyclopedia, in the entry for Africa.

> *You don't have to wait for next Trick or Treat*
> *To find yourself something that's sweet to eat*
> *And while you're at it you're on your way*
> *To finding the next clue that's hidden today·*

The clue is in the cookie jar or bag.

> *If you want to know the next clue's site*
> *I can help, and shed a little light.*
> *In fact, if you'll look for a lot of light*
> *You won't have to hunt all through the night.*

The clue is among the supply of spare light bulbs in the closet.

Since kids love being the keepers of secrets and mysteries, and the ones who wield power, your child will probably be eager to be the next hider of the treasure and clues. You may have to supply her with the treasure to hide for the next seeker, but after that she should be glad to write the next set of clues for someone else to seek out and decipher.

Watson, the game's afoot!

Paging Western Union

Ask your child to make up a telegram that might have been sent from one character in a book to another. You have to guess who the sender and recipient are supposed to be. Kids love to quiz their parents, and while your child is making up each stumper for you, he'll be exercising his creativity muscles and discovering how much fun reading can be.

For a more challenging variation, particularly for older kids, let the telegram be from a character in one book to a character in a different book. How about a telegram from Huck Finn telling Jo of *Little Women* that she could get ideas for more stories to write and sell if she went rafting with him? Or a telegram from Rudyard Kipling's Mowgli to Winnie the Pooh letting him know he could catch plenty of heffalumps in the jungle?

Later, your child can play this game with his friends, and they can take turns writing the telegrams and guessing the senders and recipients. If you have more than one child, they can play the game together.

"Ransom" Stories

You know the form of the classic ransom note—it's spelled out either with letters or whole words cut from magazines or newspapers and pasted onto a piece of paper. Your child can write a short story in the same manner. He'll need to assemble one or more sheets of typing or construction paper, as well as scissors, glue or paste, and some old magazines that can be cut up. Magazines are much neater to work with than newspapers.

Looking over the available words, he cuts out and pastes down whole words wherever possible, spelling out words letter by letter when necessary, to create a short story. The stories are likely to be choppy, not polished, and somewhat lacking in literary finesse. But since the creator is confined to the words in the magazines (unless he wants to painstakingly paste each word in place letter by letter), in their own way these stories require more creativity than a story written from scratch.

Jigsaw Stories

For these stories your child needs paper, a pen, pencil, or typewriter, scissors, and an envelope for each page of paper of the story.

She starts by writing an original story down on paper. It may fit on one page or take twenty, but when it's written she cuts up each page into a jigsaw pattern. She may want to cut freehand, or she may find it's easier to draw a jigsaw-puzzle pattern on the back of each sheet first and then cut along the lines. Either way, each page's cut-up pieces go into a separate envelope so the pieces of one page don't get mixed in with the pieces of another. She also should label each envelope with its appropriate page number when the pieces go into it.

Now she gives or sends the puzzle to a friend, who has to put the pieces together to read the story. (If your child plans in advance to send this story to Jan, she can write the story *about* Jan, which will be a big treat for Jan after opening each envelope and assembling the pages. Then the next story can be about Chris, and sent to Chris.)

Silly Stories

This fun game for two or more requires someone—your child— to write a story first, and therein lies the creativity-stretching. You'll probably want to write the first story to show your child how it's done, or you can use the sample below, but after that your child should write the stories. The story, which should be short, has lots of blanks to fill in. It might go something like this:

One day _____ a (person we all know) was walking down the street when she found a(n) _____ (color) _____ (noun). She couldn't believe her good luck at finding such a(n) _____ (adjective) _____ (noun), so she ran to the police to report it, hoping nobody would claim it within _____ (number) days and then she could keep it. The most amazing thing about what she found was that it was _____ (adjective).

When she got it to the police station, she found it was a magic _____ (noun), because it _____ed (verb) when she _____ed(verb) it. The policeman said, "I never saw such a _____ (adjective) thing in all my _____ (number) years on the force. You'd better take that to _____ (place) before it _____s (verb)."

He even reported it to the newspapers, and they wrote a _____ (adjective) story all about it. Some TV producers made the story into a TV movie. The part of our heroine was played by _____ (famous person). People flocked to our heroine's house to see the _____ (adjective) thing. People came from _____ (number) states as far away as _____ (place). Our heroine got famous and rich, charging people _____ (number) dollars to see the thing and earning a total of _____ (number) dollars.

After the first story is written (or you use the one above), you play the game like this: There are at least two players, and more is fine. One person has the story in front of her, and a pencil or pen. She asks the other players, in turn, for the part of speech that is called for to fill in each blank. She does not give them any hint of what the story is about. She simply asks for a noun, verb, or adjective, as required, filling in the words supplied by the other players in the appropriate blanks. When all the blanks have been filled in she reads the story aloud, complete with the filled-in blanks. If your child wants to keep playing this game, she'll need to write more stories, complete with blanks to fill in, and that's fine with you—right?

Once Upon a Tommy

One way to encourage kids to write is to get them to write stories about each other. If you have two (or more) kids, get each to write a story about the other. If you have an only child, get him to write stories about his friends, suggesting that they reciprocate—who wouldn't want to be the star of a story?

If your son, Tommy, writes a story about his best friend, Matt, riding the first spaceship to Venus, Matt may in turn write a story about Tommy as the youngest cowboy in the West. On a less fantastic level, if Tommy writes about Matt organizing a sidewalk sale and earning lots of money for the club, Matt might write about Tommy getting to meet and shake hands with the President of the United States. So put your child's brain to work writing stories about his siblings, friends, classmates, or neighbors.

Once he's written the story he can put the paper between two sheets of construction paper, with the title on the front sheet, book-style, and present it to the friend it's written about.

Proverbially Speaking

Your child is probably familiar with Aesop's fables—stories with animals as characters that brought proverbs to life. Your child, too, can write fables that illustrate proverbs. Have her decide on a proverb or other moral to personify through characters in a story. Then she can start thinking of the one she'll write to accomplish that goal. The story's characters can be animals, like Aesop's, though they can just as easily be people. There is no set length she needs to aim for—just as long as it takes to tell the story that illustrates the moral. Besides practicing writing, she may even take the proverbs to heart!

"Dear Grown-Up Me"

Even kids who don't keep diaries, don't want to write letters to Grandma, and seem destined to leave little of their childhood in print can sometimes be persuaded to write letters to themselves.

He can write a letter to his grown-up self, one he might address, "Dear Grown-Up Me," to be opened and read many years later. This letter should evoke both memories and feelings. Of course, the contents are up to your child, but my suggestion would be a long letter describing his room, your house, the neighborhood, the school, his friends, and the highlights of the year, including his triumphs and tribulations, joys and sorrows.

Start with simple stuff: paint and wallpaper. Paint and wallpaper? Yes. Evoke the colors and textures of the room, the house, the neighborhood. He may think he'll always remember, that the house will always be there, but it's remarkable the things we forget, and you might sell the house or at least redecorate it. He may remember the Disney wallpaper and forget the one with the clown motif; he may remember the yellow wall paint he had from age thirteen to eighteen but forget the hideous green paint he picked out himself and was stuck with from age nine to thirteen.

Was there a secret place down by the railroad tracks that was "his spot," which you never even knew about? Did the wisteria by the back porch, which gave up the ghost when your son turned ten, hold a special memory for him? He may forget these things, important as they were at the time, without a reminder in writing. And that reminder should include some verbal cues to triggers—emotions as well.

What about remembrances of emotions? Your child needs to record those memories: the events, feelings, milestones, and markers of childhood and adolescence. The first time your son pitched a sandlot or Little League no-hitter—or struck out. The first time your daughter climbed to the top of the rope in gym— only to have her triumph marred when a classmate yelled, "What a hole in your gym outfit! Pretty pink panties!" That first crush on a teacher, a movie star, a classmate. The fear that gripped your daughter before she went onstage in the lead in the school play—and the glow she felt when her best friend tossed a dozen daisies to her at curtain call.

Who was it that bested your son in the spelling bee, the year he was one of two left on stage? What word tripped him up, and how did he feel as he stumbled and erred? What was it the boys said, and how did he feel, the year they all had to take Home Ec and he won an award for best cake? It'll all come back to him if he writes it down in the form of a letter to himself and preserves it:

Dear Grown-Up Me,
    "You'll never believe what Katy O'Donnell said in school today when three other boys and I...."

Chapter 2

Artistic Endeavors

Of course, not all creativity involves words. Your child can exercise creativity with crafts and artwork, and he can do it even if he isn't a Rembrandt-in-training. There are plenty of arts and crafts projects that don't even require the ability to draw a straight line, but they'll still exercise those creativity muscles.

Very Personalized Stationery

Your child may be much more inspired to write those letters to Grandma and Grandpa if he has his very own unique stationery. Personalized stationery also makes a great, low-cost gift for friends, of which your child can proudly say, "I made it myself!"

What he'll need depends on how he wants to decorate the stationery. At a minimum, he'll need white typing paper (or copier paper in ivory or another pale color) and crayons or colored markers. He can either write, "From the desk of _____ (name)," "From _____," or even his full name and address. Other popular sentiments are "A note from _____" and "Just for you…from _____," though he can certainly feel free to use some other heading on the page if he prefers.

"A note from" stationery is often illustrated with a musical note—corny but cute. Girls frequently draw flowers on their stationery. Sunrises and clouds are popular too. Monograms are suitable for either sex.

If you have a copying machine at home and your child plans to run off multiple copies, using colored crayons or markers is unimportant. In fact, black will copy better than some colors, unless, of course, your photocopier reproduces colors.

If you are using a copier to run off multiple copies, your child can cut a small picture out of a magazine, preferably in black and white, and paste it onto the original sheet of stationery. Your child can use pictures of horses, cats, dogs, or other animals, kids at play or reading, sports motifs, flowers, trees, or anything else he finds appealing. If not making multiple copies on a photocopier, girls may want to cut out sections of paper lace dollies and glue them onto the corners of the stationery.

Besides being a creative craft in its own right and providing incentive for the child to write more of those all-important letters to Grandma, just impelling the child to write letters to *anyone* is a good thing. The more he writes—to relatives, friends, or anyone—the more he's expressing himself and learning to organize his thoughts by putting them down on paper.

String Paintings

For this project you will need to assemble in advance: tempera paints, paper, lengths of string from one to two feet long, and something like newspaper to cover and protect the work surface.

Your help will be needed on this one the first time, and thereafter as well with younger artists. The first thing you need to do is spread out newspaper, plastic, or some other paint-proofer to protect your table or other work surface. Then fold the piece of paper in half and open it again. Dip a length of string into one of the paint colors and hold it above the paint till it's done dripping. All of the string should be covered with paint *except the end that the child is holding.* Lay it down on one side of the paper little by little, letting it settle into loops and twists and curves, with the unpainted end sticking out over the edge of the paper. Then do another string the same way, probably in a different color, and keep going till you're satisfied with the number of strings you've laid down.

Your child may want to have five strings, all of one color, or ten, each of a different color, or any other combination. Remember, though, that all the strings should be laid down on *one side* of the paper and all the clean ends should extend past the paper.

When the artist is content with the number of strings and colors, she folds the paper in half again, pressing down, but not too hard, on the strings. Then she pulls each string out, one at a time, while still pressing the paper down.

When all the strings have been removed, she unfolds the paper and observes the resulting work of art.

Scratch Paintings

For this project you will need to assemble in advance: paper (you can use ordinary typing paper, though heavier paper is better), assorted colors of paint, a black crayon, and a coin. The project is easy; your child can do it with minimal verbal guidance and no help in the actual procedure. Here is how he proceeds:

Cover the entire page with color—lines, stripes, swirls, circles, crescents, zigzags, or aimless, random squiggles and whorls—anything will do. Use as many different colors as you want, in any random pattern you want, though it's better not to have any one color cover too broad or solid an area. When the whole page is covered in colored paint, cover all the color with black crayon. Solid black. Thick black. Lots and lots of black.

Take the coin and lightly scratch lines, swoops, swirls, and whirls all across the surface of the painting. As you do, the black will be scratched away, revealing the colors underneath. One swoopy line will reveal a myriad of colors, and the effect in some cases can be quite spectacular.

Variation: Instead of drawing random designs with the coin, draw lines that form an actual picture, or your initials or name. The house, flower, animal, or whatever you draw will be multi-hued and striking because of the pattern of color underneath.

Phone-Wire Sculpture

If yours is one of the families with odd lengths of phone wire lying around (and if it isn't, you can buy the stuff at the hardware store for very little money), you have sculpting material on hand for a child old enough to work with wire, and possibly a knife. Or, if she's old enough to have sufficient fine muscle control to work with small, thin wires, but not old enough to use a knife responsibly, you can do all the knifework, leaving the rest of the sculpting to your child.

Sculpting phone wire? Yes. Here's the story: Phone wire comes insulated in an outer covering, often beige or grey, which can be peeled or sliced away. Removing the outer covering will reveal four strands of wire within, covered in their own insulation—one is red, one green, one yellow, and one black. The wires bend very easily, can be cut (with scissors, knife, pliers, or wire cutters), and hold their shape faithfully once they have been twisted and bent into a given shape. Your child can shape the wire into a little dog, a house, or a person.

Two or more lengths of wire can be twisted together so that a red roof can be attached to a black house, or different colors can be interlocked for a free-form sculpture. By giving a house four sides or a dog four legs so the sculpture has a good base, you child can enable it to stand up. The wire is strong enough to hold its own weight.

Your child can sculpt recognizable designs fashioned after items in the real world, such as stars, cats, and boats, or abstract designs that play with form and color. She can even craft a mini-community—houses, people, pets, trees, and rudimentary cars—which is fun on its own, or can lead to a session of make-believe, with interaction among the residents of the community.

When your child runs around the house in overdrive, perhaps you've been known to make the comment, "Boy, that kid is wired today!" This sculpting medium will give a whole new meaning to that phrase!

Paste-a-Pasta

For this activity you need a selection of shaped pasta (spirals, clamshells, elbows, bows, and whatever else you can acquire), a cigar box or similar hinge-lidded container, glue, spray paint (silver or gold are recommended), and two or three square feet of pretty fabric. You'll end up with a child who's exercising his creative abilities; your child will end up with a pretty box suitable for giving to Grandma or a friend as a gift.

The child glues the pasta to the top, and perhaps the sides, of the box. He can use a random pattern, create a picture or design with the pasta, or even spell the name or write the initials of the intended recipient. (This is even easier to do with alphabet macaroni than by forming the recipient's name with elbows or other forms of pasta.)

After the glue has dried, the child spray paints the box and pasta till it's all glittery silver, gold, or other color. When the paint is dry, he lines the box with the fabric. (If desired, and if you have batting in your sewing kit, he can use some as padding between the fabric and the box. The result is usable as a jewelry, knicknacks, or treasures box.

Life in the Comics

Ask your child to draw a series of comic-strip pictures depicting a typical day in her life. No punch line is needed. If this resembles a comic strip, it's more along the lines of a serialized one than a funny one.

Of course, if she has a talent for humor and draws a truly funny comic-book-style depiction of daily life, praise her; but don't criticize if you get a rather pedestrian depiction of tooth brushing, breakfast eating, classwork, lunch, homework, dinner, TV, and bedtime in six or ten panels with nothing particularly funny about them. Your child is still exploring creative ways to look at and depict mundane activities.

You're likely to learn something from her pictures, though: that her bus driver is an eight-foot commando in a hardhat, or that the teacher is a two-headed creature with eyes in the back of both heads!

Re-Designing Child

A simple pencil eraser, if used carefully, will usually erase the ink from newsprint. Success on slick magazine paper is chancier but sometimes possible. Now that you know this, you—and your child—know how to redesign anyone whose picture appears in the paper, or possibly a magazine.

Erase the face from an ad for Barbie and make her look completely different. Do the same for the President or First Lady, Oprah, Geraldo, Sting, Tammy Wynette, Jean-Claude van Damme, or Julia Roberts. Or Barney, Big Bird, Donald Duck, or the Roadrunner.

Of course, your child can draw a moustache on Tammy Wynette or long curls on Jean-Claude van Damme, but a creative and not ridiculous, believable change is applicable here too. What would Julia look like with different lips? Geraldo with a different nose? Tammy with different hair? Oprah with different eyes? What about a bald Hulk Hogan? Michael Jackson in a business suit, carrying an attaché case? The power conferred on your child by that eraser and pen or pencil is awesome.

Themed Collages

For this project you will need to assemble in advance: one large sheet of heavy paper (such as construction paper) or light-colored cardboard, glue or paste, scissors, and magazines. Optional: old photos you don't want to keep intact, old greeting cards or picture postcards you don't mind cutting up, paper lace doilies, crayons, and colored marking pens.

Of course, any collage is fun to make, but choosing a theme makes the collage more special. The theme can be animals, or a particular animal, such as cats, dogs, or horses, happiness, family, birthdays, seasons, holidays, sports, food, or anything else that appeals to your child and of which there are sufficient pictures around.

The pictures can come from magazines, postcards, greeting cards, photos, or any other source you have available. The child cuts out the parts of the pictures he wants to use and pastes them down on the heavy paper or cardboard. He will probably want to overlap some of the pictures over others. Your child may want to interweave with the pictures any of the following: shapes cut out of construction paper, little pictures he's drawn on paper, words that he's cut from magazines suitable to the theme of the collage, paper lace doilies, or whatever else is on hand that comes to mind as suitable.

Stained Glass Windows—Version 1

For this version of stained glass windows you'll need to assemble the following materials: one piece of onionskin typing paper, one piece of colored construction paper, colored markers, glue or paste, and scissors. Your child proceeds as follows:

Cut out various irregular-shaped pieces from within the construction paper. These do not need to be standard shapes such as triangles, squares, and circles, but can be free-form cuts. The one rule, though, is not to cut over to the edge of the paper at any point. Keep an untouched border around the edge. When you're finished cutting, the paper will probably have about as much area removed from it as remains.

Now apply paste or glue to the remaining area of construction paper and glue it to the onionskin paper. Using colored markers, color in that part of the onionskin that is exposed through the cutouts in the construction paper. Your stained glass window is finished and ready to be hung. Do this by attaching it to the pane of a window that gets a lot of sunlight, and let the sun light up the colors.

Stained Glass Windows—Version 2

For this version of a stained glass window you need to assemble the following materials in advance: old crayons, waxed paper, black construction paper, newspaper, scissors, Scotch tape, a grater, iron, and ironing board. Since a grater and an iron are involved, depending on your child's age, more of your participation may be needed in this project than in the version above. Here's how your child proceeds:

Remove the paper labels from the crayons and grate the crayons with the grater, allowing crumbles of all the different colors to mix together. Turn the iron on low (dry, not steam), and put five layers of newspaper down on the ironing board. Then lay a piece of waxed paper on the newspaper. Tear off a piece of waxed paper approximately the same size as the sheet of black construction paper.

Sprinkle the crayon crumbles all over the waxed paper, distributing them fairly evenly and not too thickly. Now put another piece of waxed paper of the same size on the top of the crayon crumbles above the first piece. The iron (still on low) should be warmed up by now. Iron the waxed paper till the grated crayon bits melt and run together. Turn off the iron. Set the crayoned waxed paper aside and let it cool.

Meanwhile, cut shapes out of the black construction paper, being careful to leave the edges uncut. When at least as much of the paper has been cut away as remains, tape the construction paper to the front of the crayoned waxed paper. The colored waxed paper will show through the cutouts in the black construction paper. Hang the whole thing in a sunny window for maximum effect.

Stamp of Approval

Suppose your child were postmaster general? Suppose there were no restrictions on what could be depicted on a postage stamp? What would she like to see as the motif of next year's stamps?

Ask your child to design a number of stamps. These may depict anything or anyone she wants. She can honor a current or past political or entertainment figure, family member or any other person.

Of course, stamps can depict abstract concepts too: Patriotism and freedom are certainly fitting ideals to be featured on postage, but if your child chooses one of these, or some other abstract idea to grace next year's stamps, she'll need to draw a picture that illustrates the concept. Remember, the design of a stamp encompasses more than just its picture. Where does the denomination go? The words?

When she's done planning next year's stamp issues, maybe she'd like to take a crack at designing some new coins and currency. A twenty-five-dollar bill? A twenty cent coin? A design for a new, smaller nickel? Or a larger dime? How about one that's easier to distinguish from a penny at the bottom of a change purse?

It's a Wrap

With a supply of paint or a sponge and inkpad, and brown package-wrapping paper or butcher paper, your child can design wrapping paper that will delight Grandma and Grandpa on the next gift-giving occasion almost as much as the contents.

Your child can:

• Draw on the paper.

• Using fingerpaints, leave handprints or footprints all over the paper.

• Sign or print his name all over the paper.

• Cut a sponge into a design, dip it into an inkpad, and stamp the design all over the paper. By using two or more sponges and two or more colors of ink, he can create an interesting pattern.

• Cut out an assortment of comic strip animals (you may need to collect them over a week or so in order to have enough), and paste them onto the brown paper. If desired, a coat of shellac can be applied over the cutouts to keep the ink from smudging. Use the Sunday comics if your paper doesn't run strips in color during the week.

Hold It!

What do you hold paper clips in? Pens and pencils? The spare change you're accumulating? Other bits and pieces? Your child can decorate various containers to make them appealing.

Start either with a can with the top removed (check for sharp edges, discarding the can if you find any) or a milk jug whose top half has been cut off (probably by you again, since careful work with a very sharp knife is needed).

Your child can decorate the can with wrapping paper, construction paper she's drawn on or has glued glitter onto in a decorative design, or in any other creative way. A translucent white milk jug can have shells glued onto it, glitter in a pattern, or even decorative buttons. It can be painted with paint or nailpolish. She can cut pictures out of comic strips or comic books, gluing them onto the container and covering the comic cutouts with a coat of clear nail polish. But by no means should your child feel restricted to just the suggestions above. Her creativity can extend to the materials she uses as well as the designs and patterns she creates with them.

Your child can keep some of the finished containers—they might even help her keep her room more organized, with marbles in one container, jacks in another, pennies in one, and pencils in another—or they make good gifts at birthdays or Christmastime.

Seasonal Greetings

Whether the season is Christmas or Valentine's Day, or a birthday is being celebrated, here's an idea for recycling old greeting cards that won't bankrupt your child's piggy, costing only the price of a sheet of construction paper, a little glue, some ink or crayon, and scissors.

Have your child cut out pictures from old greeting cards, and then, folding a piece of construction paper in half to simulate a card, he pastes down the cutout pictures. He has the following options:

• Cut out and paste various pictures overlapping each other, collage-style. Write "happy birthday," "season's greetings," or some other suitable greeting on the front.

• Cut out and paste one suitable picture (such as a Christmas tree, Santa, a heart, Cupid, a birthday cake, or balloons) and draw around it using crayons or markers. Complete the picture in ink or crayon, for example, by drawing a group of people gathered around the cake, or a roof under Santa with a chimney adjacent, and write a suitable greeting as well. Either way, he writes a greeting, a verse, or other suitable sentiment inside the card.

Half a Rembrandt

For this activity you'll need a picture—preferably something that is not a portrait or an abstract painting or drawing, and definitely a picture that your child has not seen before. If you have a coffee-table book reproducing famous art, you're off to a good start. If not, perhaps you can borrow one from the library or find a reproduction of a good-quality painting or drawing in a magazine.

Cover half the picture with anything handy—a piece of typing paper, a dish towel, a book—and show the visible half to your child. Then ask her what might be in the covered half of the picture.

If your child has artistic talent, you can reproduce the

picture on a color photocopier. Cut out half, paste it down on a sheet of blank white typing paper, and ask the child to draw or paint the missing half.

For most kids it's sufficient to ask them to just describe the items, probably including their shapes, colors, and sizes, to be found in the missing half of the picture. You do want to ask, though, what visual clues in the existing half other picture gave them the idea that a cow, a woman in a lace-trimmed dress, an older man, a banana, or a bicyclist might be depicted in the missing half. In the process, your child may absorb some principles of design.

When your child has finished describing—or drawing—the missing half, show her the complete original. No matter how spectacularly different from the original painting your child's guesses are, remind her that there are no wrong answers in this game.

Chapter 3

Writing Aloud

Not all stories are written. Oral storytelling has a long and honorable history. Traditionally, campfires go hand in hand with tall tales, for instance. Ghost stories, too, are often created aloud rather than on paper. Such legendary heroes as Paul Bunyan, Pecos Bill, and Mike Fink were originally created by writers who "wrote" aloud, not on paper. These beloved characters didn't have their exploits recorded till well after their tales had first been told.

Writing aloud serve many purposes for kids as well. For one thing, some kinds who love spinning yarns will balk at being asked to sit down and literally write their stories out. A child who thinks spinning a yarn is a great way to pass fifteen minutes may think that writing the same story down feels more like schoolwork.

A child too young to write neatly or spell well will find that the struggle to figure out the spelling of every other word hampers the creative process. When you have to first think of how to spell "elephant," then how to make an *E*, you're not going to have the same interest in writing a story about a little elephant as you would in just *telling* the story.

So let the child just tell the story—to you, to his siblings or friends, or into a tape recorder. In fact, there are activities in this section that *require* that the stories be written aloud. But in addition to these, encourage your child to write other stories aloud if he feels that putting pen to paper is too much like doing homework.

She can follow one of the time-honored traditions and write a ghost story or a tall tale, or he can write any kind of story at all, telling it to you or another person, or dictating it on tape. If he does write a tall tale he can have it be about a folk hero whose exploits he's already familiar with, or can invent a character or even write about himself.

If your child tends to tell tall tales about himself anyway, passing them off as truth, here's an opportunity to help him gently distinguish between reality and fantasy, lying and fiction-writing!

Progressive Alphabet Stories

This game requires at least two players, and the more the merrier. The first player leads off with any sentence at all, starting with any letter of the alphabet he chooses. The sillier the sentence the better, just to make the game fun, but silliness is not a requirement.

Let's say the opening sentence is: Fred the flamingo wanted to join the orchestra, but his beak got in the way of his playing his flute.

The next player's sentence must begin with the letter *that follows the letter at the beginning of the previous sentence.* Since the first sentence began with an *F,* the second sentence must begin with a *G.*

Play continues this way for twenty-six sentences—one for each of the twenty-six letters of the alphabet. (After the Z sentence, the next sentence begins with *A.*) When twenty-six sentences have been created and play is back to the letter before the one that started the game, the game is over. (If you wish, you can choose to eliminate the X and Z sentences.)

Progressive Cliffhangers

Another type of progressive story, again requiring at least two players, is the Progressive Cliffhanger. In this game the first player starts off by spinning a story about anything at all. Unlike the game above, players aren't limited to one sentence each. No player should carry the narrative for too long, however, but should let the next player have a turn fairly quickly.

The point in the story at which one player turns over the storytelling to the next is at a cliffhanger of some sort. Maybe our hero has just discovered a mysterious package, has lost his pet turtle, is trapped in an underground passage, or is lost in a secret hallway. At that point the storyteller turns the action over to the next player.

The next player picks up the thread of the story and carries on till he gets to a suitable place for turning it over to the next one. Again, this may be at a crucial, mysterious, or suspenseful point in the action.

These stories tend to change location often. A story that started out under the Willises' back porch might quickly change locale to the schoolyard, then to a secret garden behind the Martinsons' house, then to NASA headquarters, then Jupiter, and finally the police station. There is no preset ending to one of these stories. The game is over when the story comes to a logical conclusion, gets mired in too many details, all the loose ends have been wrapped up, or the players decide it has gone on long enough and it's time to start a new story.

Describe-a-Thing

The ability to create an evocative description is a must for any writer, but even someone with no literary aspirations will find her life improved by the ability to describe an object, person, place, or event better than just adequately.

Here are three activities that involve describing things:

• Ask your child to describe any object within sight. This is not a game in which she earns points, but you should definitely praise her for description that is precise or poetic. For instance, is it simply a small box, or a box quite similar in size to a deck of cards? Is it just green, or the color of a stormy sea? Does it have a dented corner, a jewel worthy of a queen, three hinges, or a flower painted on it that would cheer up anyone feeling down? Praise your child for all details if accurate or evocative.

• Ask your child to do the same again with an object that is out of sight. Here her ability to recall objects and envision them comes into play.

If your child is consistently unable to describe objects out of sight, it's possible she is more receptive to auditory rather than visual information. This is not to say she shouldn't pay attention to the world around her, but her inability to picture objects clearly may not result from her failing to pay attention. She may be one of the minority of people who relate more to what they hear than what they see. Try asking her to describe a sound instead of a visible object and see if you don't get a better description.

• If you have two kids or your child has a friend visiting, have one describe something—preferably an object and not a person—while the other tries to draw it. This could be something the child has seen, or something she is making up in her own mind. It should not be something in the room with you, or something with which the child doing the drawing is familiar.

Of course the one with the artistic chore is not likely to reproduce an exact copy of what the other child is describing, but it's a great experiment to see how close the "artist" comes.

Cut-Out Stories

Here's a way to get younger kids involved in creating characters and "writing" a little tale about them, even if the kids aren't ready to fabricate whole stories with plots, neatly wrapped endings, and all the other niceties of well-crafted fiction.

Go through a magazine you don't mind having cut up, and ask your child to point to picture of two or three people who look interesting. (If he points to pictures in advertisements, this is fine. It also doesn't matter whether the pictures are photos or line drawings.)

Now ask him a little about each person in the photo. Tell the child to feel free to make up all the details; make it clear you are seeking fiction here, not reality. What is the name of each person whose picture you cut out? If an adult, does he or she work for a living? What does he or she do? How old is he or she? Does he or she have a family? Might the different people you've cut out be related? Elicit as much information about each person as the child is comfortable making up.

Now ask the child to make up a short story about the people. A really little child might tell a very short story without much plot, but you didn't really expect him to craft a Pulitzer Prize winner at age four, did you? He's learning—today he can make up a little bit of information about the people in the pictures, tomorrow he'll write a whole story with a beginning, middle, and end, characterization, plot, and a resolution.

After starting over again with a new story, if the child is still attentive, "introduce" two characters from different stories to each other. "What would happen if the daddy from the first story met the plumber from the second story?" You can even suggest a plot twist: "Suppose the plumber went to the daddy's house to fix some pipes and found something spooky in the basement?" or "Suppose the plumber were fixing the daddy's pipes and found an old trunk in a back corner of the basement? Suppose the daddy said, 'I don't know what's in it. It was there when we moved into the house.' Then suppose they opened it. What do you think they found inside?"

A Bowl Full of Improv

You're probably familiar with the concept of improv, that is, improvisational theatre. Someone gives actors a concept and they have to act out a scene involving the suggested characters in the given situation. Here's a game that's an exercise in improv. It can be played by just one child or multiple players. You will do the initial preparation.

You'll need three bowls, a pen or pencil, and a fair number of slips of paper or index cards. I'd suggest a minimum of twenty-one in a one-player game, more in a multi-player game. Use three of the cards (or slips of paper) as labels for the three bowls. Label them "People," "Places," and "Situations."

On the remaining slips of paper, you're going to write who or what some people, places, and situations might be. For people, you might write "The President of the U.S.," "a dentist," "a teacher," "an aunt," "a train conductor," or "an astronaut." For places you might write "Disneyland," "work," "on a bus," "in a restaurant," "undersea," and "in a swimming pool." For situations, perhaps, "has no money," "frustrated in what he or she is trying to do," "amnesia," "has flat tire," "arrives in church after sermon has started," and "stuck in traffic."

Let's assume a one-player game for the moment. This could be either one child playing the game herself or several kids who've each agreed to take a turn at playing solo. The player draws one slip from each bowl. Perhaps she winds up with "dentist," "Disneyland," and "has no money." Now she has to play the part of a dentist who, at Disneyland, finds he or she has no money in his or her pocket.

Will the dentist report a pickpocketing to the police? Plead for free admission to the rides? Offer to perform future dental work in exchange for some money now?

The scene may last just a few seconds or quite a few minutes, depending both on the child's improvisational activities and on how fertile a field has been provided by the particular ingredients she's picked. Some combinations are richer in possibilities than others.

For two or more players there are two ways to proceed.

• *Version One:* The child picks three slips of paper, as above, which will determine which part she plays, where the action takes place, and what the situation is, just as in the one-player version above. The other player or players can choose what parts they are going to play, but they need to fit in logically with the character, setting, and situation that the first player drew from the bowls.

If Matt is a football player in a classroom, who can't find his shoes, it would seem logical that this football player is a college or high school student, so one of the other players might decide to be a teacher or professor, and other players might be fellow students.

Then again, if Matt can't find his shoes, perhaps Amanda wants to play the part of a police officer or security guard. Or other players may have other ideas for characters they could logically assume.

• *Version Two:* This version, for two or more players, involves more slips in the "People" bowl than in the "Places" and "Situations" bowls, and requires each player to pick a slip from the "People" bowl. Only one will also pick from "Places" and "Situations." She is the main character, but the others will interact with her according to the characters they have picked.

Amanda might pick "salesman," "factory," and "the pastor is visiting." Matt, the only other player, might pick "chicken farmer." (Characters do not necessarily have to be the same sex as the players.) Somehow, Matt and Amanda need to work out a scene involving a salesman who either works for or calls on a factory where pastor is visiting and a chicken farmer can also be found on this particular day. (Maybe the factory manufactures chicken coops? Maybe the pastor is a racing pigeon fancier? Pastors have hobbies too, you know.)

With more than three players, it is strongly recommended that any beyond the first two players be allowed to select characters of their own choosing, not from pre-selected characters in a bowl. Otherwise you get an impossible agglomeration of characters that's difficult to blend together in a workable scene.

In yet another variation, you can omit one or two of the bowls. Now, instead of being required to portray a cashless dentist at Disneyland, the player might just be required to be a cashless dentist, or a dentist at Disneyland, or a cashless person of unspecified identity at Disneyland. Some kids do better when all the elements are laid out for them; others do better with less structure.

Situation Grab-bag

Here's a game, related to "A Bowl Full of Improv," that a group of kids or kids and parents can play together. Everyone needs a pen or pencil and a piece of paper. Each player writes down a situation without telling the others what he's writing. Here are some examples:

• You're in the supermarket when suddenly a skunk runs down the aisle.

• The mailman brings you a huge package and it isn't even your birthday.

• You step into your backyard and see a spinning disk with glowing lights coming down from the sky.

• The president decides he wants an advisor on problems of

ordinary kids. He picks an ordinary kid to advise him—you! Suddenly you're asked to move to Washington with your family.

• You plant a package of giant sunflower seeds and one sunflower grows so big, thick, and tall you can't even see the top of it. You wonder if there's a giant at the top like Jack and the beanstalk.

• The local newspaper sends you to the Superbowl to interview the players' kids—but you have to change planes in Dallas and you miss your connecting flight.

Everyone folds up his piece of paper with the situation written on it. On the outside of the paper, everyone writes his initials. Drop the papers into a bowl or hat. Everyone then draws out a piece of paper and, without unfolding the paper, makes sure they haven't drawn their own. Anyone who has drawn his own paper should trade with another player. When no one has his own paper, choose who will go first.

Only that person opens his paper. After taking a minute to read the situation and think about it, he starts telling a story based on the situation written on the paper he has drawn. When he has finished his story, decide who will go next. Continue till all have had a turn. Nobody opens his paper and reads his situation till it's his turn.

Variation: Instead of writing a situation on his piece of paper before dropping it into the bowl, each player provides an opening sentence. Whoever picks that piece of paper must begin his story with that sentence.

Hand Me a Line

Like "A Bowl Full of Improv," this game expands your child's creativity through improvisational acting. In "Hand Me a Line," no preparation is needed. You may want to think of some lines ahead of time if you know you're going to play "Hand Me a

Line" with your child, but you can also be as spontaneous as your child will have to be.

You start the scene by giving a line to your child. Then she has to answer you in character, as the person your line has suggested she is. For instance, if you start the proceedings by saying, "Good afternoon, Ms. Beckett. I'm Dr. Monroe. Now what seems to be wrong with that leg?" your child knows she's expected to play the part of Ms. Beckett, a patient in a doctor's office, who has a leg problem.

On the other hand, if you say, "How did this carousel get into the air and where are we heading?" you and your child are both riding a carousel that's airborne.

You can choose fantasy situations, plausible situations, or even some involving actual people you know or know of. Of course, when your child responds to your opening line you'll be drawn more deeply into the scene. Keep it going till the scene comes to a logical conclusion or you're stuck. Just a few lines might be exchanged, or the scene could play for ten minutes or longer. Your child exercises her creativity by inventing dialogue and keeping in character, devising and spontaneously carrying out the scene as it plays. But after she's played the game a few times she may want to feed you the lines. Now she's exercising even more creativity, thinking of the initial dialogue as well as carrying the dialogue forward once the scene is established.

"You Put the Words in My Mouth"

Prepare for this game by writing a number of words on index cards (or slips of paper), one word per card, making sure they're words the child is familiar with, yet are not words that are likely to pop up in any old sentence. They do not have to be obscure, outrageous, or off-the-wall, but neither should they be "a," "and," or "you." "Taxicab," "refrigerator," "ecstatic," or "howl" would do fine. You might want to start by making up ten of these cards.

You and your child should pick two characters and carry on a conversation in character. Weave the words on those cards into the conversation. Decide in advance on how often one of the words is to be interpolated into the dialogue. You might say each person has to use one of the words in every other sentence.

How you decide the nature of your characters is up to you. You can use the "people" bowl from Plot-in-a-Pot (see page 17), take turns deciding in advance what each dialogue will be about, or utilize any other means that suits you.

Say you agree that you're playing the part of a teacher who's failing a football playing student in geometry. Your son, Matt, is playing the part of the football player. You agree that Matt will start the dialogue.

Matt: Is there any way I can get extra credit to boost my grade? (He picks a card. He's going to need to use the word on that card in his next sentence. The word is *isolate*.)

You: If you'd study harder you'd pass, and your football career wouldn't be in jeopardy. (You pick a card to use in your next sentence. The word is *measles*.)

Matt: Are you isolating me for this treatment? I bet you didn't fail any of the other players. (That's two sentences, so he picks another card for use in his next sentence. The word is *circus*.)

You: I was ready to fail Bobby, but after he came down with the measles he dropped off the team anyhow.

Matt: If I can't play football, I might as well run away and join the circus.

You: The way you carry on in class, you'd be a perfect clown. (you pick a card.)

Note that Matt used a variant verb form of *isolate*, "isolating." A player picking *run* might say, "I ran" or "You saw her running." A player picking *potato* could legitimately say, "I don't care for potatoes."

It is not necessary, or even desirable, to keep the dialogue serious. The mere requirement of weaving words into the dialogue means that more than just improvisation is at work here, and sometimes the results are certifiably hysterical.

I Want to Sell You a Kangaroo

This pleasant, low-key, noncompetitive game engenders creativity as well as the ability to think on one's feet. It requires two players, a salesperson and a customer. The right players with offbeat senses of humor can turn the game into a gigglefest, but even when played with straight faces it's a good creativity stretcher.

The customer asks the salesperson, How much for that _____?" and names an item, such as "kangaroo." The salesperson then starts a sales spiel extolling the virtues of owning a kangaroo. The price is irrelevant; the important part is that the salesperson come up with as many clever reasons for buying the item as possible. Reasons for buying a kangaroo might include that you can ride it to school if you miss the schoolbus, that you can get into its pocket to keep warm on a cold day, or that you'd have a great item to bring to school for Show and Tell.

There is no set number of items to be included in the sales pitch and no set response on the part of the customer, who is free to reply with "Okay, I'll buy it," "Not today, thank you," or some other response, as he wishes. The salesperson may only be able to think of two or three reasons the customer should buy some items, and ten or twelve for others.

There is no winner or loser, but when the salesperson has given the pitch and the customer has replied, the player who has

been the salesperson now turns around and inquires of the
player who has been'the customer, "But tell me, how much do
you want for the _____?" naming another improbable
item.

Now the tables are turned, and the other player gets to play
salesperson, offering good, persuasive, creative reasons why the
new customer should buy, for instance, a piece of driftwood, a
"dust bunny," or a partridge egg.

Make the Connection

This activity, too, requires thinking on one's feet. Chances are
you'll play it with your child, but two kids can play together as
well. Your part consists in simply naming two unrelated things.
Then your child has to find a way to connect them.

For instance, you say, "tape recorder and elephant." Your
child has to find a connection between the two. He might be brief
and fanciful, saying, "An elephant never forgets, and if it records its
thoughts with a tape recorder it can remember even easier."

Or he might get into a more complicated, longer, and more
creative connection, saying, 'If an elephant is going to be
transferred to a new zoo, the zookeeper in the old zoo could
tape-record the other elephants there. Then when the elephant
is transferred to the new zoo, the zookeeper can play back the
trumpeting sounds of the elephants in the old zoo so the
elephant doesn't get homesick."

Or it might be something as simple as, "When I go to the
zoo next time, I could tape-record the sound of the elephants to
play back when we put on the neighborhood carnival."

Connections can be made between a feather and an iron
weight, a teacher and the circus, a trampoline and a Christmas
tree, or a typewriter and garlic if a child just stretches those
creativity muscles far enough.

The Beginning, the Middle, and...

While many writers find that starting a story is the hardest part of writing, others claim that tying everything up in a neat ending is really the hardest part. The end has to be satisfactory and believable, resolving all the problems and tying up all the loose ends.

Your child, of course, probably prefers happy endings, although just as in real life, not all stories end "happily ever after." What you're asking for is an ending that accomplishes everything I mentioned above; whether it's happy or not is optional.

Your part in this activity, setting it in motion, is to start a story. In addition, by not telling a story about the Ninja Turtles, Spiderman, Cinderella, or a story that closely parallels another familiar one in theme and content, you'll teach your child, by example, how to be original, not derivative.

Knowing your child's interests and areas of knowledge, you'll be able to craft the beginning of a story likely to hold her interest, about characters and a setting that are familiar, if not from real life then from reading she's done or family stories she's heard.

Establish the story—characters, location, action, and necessary details. Get it going. Continue until you've reached a good stopping point and then bail out, leaving it to your child to pick up the story and finish it successfully.

I'm not suggesting that all that remains is to write a sentence or two. There may be much more logically left to add to the middle, and the end may take quite a few paragraphs to bring to a close that's smooth and not sudden. You're asking her to continue writing, not to synopsize the ending.

If you feel your child left loose threads dangling, by all means ask, "Yes, but what about the bear?" If you think her ending isn't believable or satisfactory, ask her questions that will prompt her to rethink it.

Crafting good endings requires both creativity and logic. This activity stimulates your child to exercise her abilities with both.

The Second Half

Read your child half a story, or even half a short book. Choose one he has never heard or read so he won't know the original ending. Then have him make up the rest of the story.

Encourage your child to elaborate on the remainder of the story with as many details as he wants, not just "They get married and live happily ever after," but details, incidents, twists of plot—any embellishments your child can come up with. He should feel free to introduce new characters too, just as long as the original conflict, situation, or question is resolved by the end.

Make it clear that you just want a good ending, not necessarily the same ending as in the original. After your child has supplied his version, by all means read the author's original to him.

If it's at all deserved, praise your child for his ingenuity, making sure he understands there was no "right" answer you were seeking in his version of the story's end. Any conclusion, no matter how far afield from the original, is good if it ties the loose ends together and resolves whatever conflict was in the story.

Initial Stories on Wheels

When you're out in the car on a trip longer than just to the corner store, instead of keeping your child busy by counting how many banks, cows, apartment buildings, or police cars you pass, ask him to write a short story written according to some very restrictive rules. Any of the following will do; some are harder than others, so pick one that's best suited to your child's abilities:

• You pick a name or word from a street sign, caution sign, highway exit marker, or other sign. Your child is to write a very short story according to the following formula: The first sentence must start with the first letter of the word or name from the sign. The second sentence starts with the second letter, the third with the third letter, and so on.

Admittedly, these "stories" will be bare-bones narratives, with only the briefest of plots and little or no embellishment, but after thinking hard, your child should be able to come up with a minimal story that fulfills the requirements.

A brief example: You pass a sign for Maple Street and challenge your son to come up with a story whose sentences begin with *M-A-P-L-E*. He says: Miss Thompson went into the haunted house that people had seen lights in. At first she was very afraid of what she would find. Presto, the door opened without her touching it. Looking inside, she saw a homeless man was living there. Everyone was happy that Miss Thompson had solved the mystery of the lights in the haunted house.

• Instead of asking him to write a story whose sentences begin with each letter of the selected word in order, ask him to write *one* sentence, with the first letter of *each word in the sentence* being each letter in order from the selected word or name. This is much harder than the version above.

• Instead of your child's story consisting of sentences that begin with each letter of a street name, pick five street signs in a row and use the first letter of each as the first letters of the sentences. Say you decide to play this game. You pass Roosevelt Avenue, Jasmine Way, Constitution Drive, Lake Avenue, and Broadway. Your child's story will consist of five sentences, the first of which will begin with an *R*, the second with a *J*, the third with a *C*, the fourth with an *L*, and the last with a *B*.

"Take My Toe"

When I was a child, some of my classmates thought it was the height of wit to sing "Take my toe/I'm a stranger in RKO" to the tune of "Take my hand/I'm a stranger in paradise." Admittedly, children's parodies are, well, childish. (The parody of "Lady of Spain" the boys sang involved her losing her pants!)

Your child, too, can write parodies. They may not be on a par with the late great Allan Sherman's work, but give your child a chance to see what she can do with taking a tune she knows and writing a set of lyrics for it that play on the original. You may be pleasantly surprised at the results, and your child will be pleased and proud if she comes up with something even halfway funny or clever.

Group Story

A fun activity for two or many more is writing a group story. Each participant thinks of two characters and decides who they are, their ages, names, occupations ("child" or "student" is fine), and as much more about them as the participants want. (If there aren't two or more kids around, a parent can engage in this activity with one child.)

Future fictioneers may well spell out elaborate details—names of characters' pets and other such trivia—but even kids destined for careers working with numbers rather than inventive stories can come up with bare-bones facts about their characters.

When all the characters (as few as four or a lot more) have

been decided on, the participants need to select a setting for the story. Does it take place in school? Arizona? A submarine under the farthest reaches of the South Pacific? A spaceship headed to Mars? The North Pole? A scout meeting? A dance? A meeting of a secret club? A treehouse?

Trying to work all the characters into something resembling a plot taking place in the agreed-upon location will be a huge challenge, and how well the participants answer it will depend in part on their ages, in part on their creative ability. Of course, if the participants are just you and your child you'll want to prompt him to come up with most of the input. You can ask questions such as "What do you think a Space Ranger was doing in Africa?" or "How do you think Jackie would have gotten along with the principal when she found herself alone with him? What would they talk about?" or "What do you suppose Evan and Rob were up to in that school gym?" You can even make some suggestions: "All four characters don't have to be in the story from the start. Suppose just Maria and Gloria were in the park at the beginning...."

Of course you can get all these stories, or the best of them, down on paper if you want, but writing them down isn't essential. It's just "writing" them—probably aloud—that's important.

Pick-a-Paragraph

For this activity you'll need a sheet of paper to cut into smaller pieces, as well as a pen or pencil for each participant, one pair of scissors, and a bowl, bag, or cap—something that can hold the cut-up pieces of paper.

After cutting the large sheet of paper into pieces just large enough to write a word on, pass out ten of these to each player. Everyone writes a different word on each of the pieces, then folds each one in half and tosses it into the bowl or other container.

Choose which player will go first. That player now picks five pieces of paper out of the container at random and devises a paragraph that uses all five words. If he wants to, he can use all five words in just one sentence, but this is not a requirement and in most cases won't be feasible.

"Laundry list" paragraphs are not acceptable. That is, if the five words Sean picks are *boy, ball, book, go,* and *train,* he is not allowed to use them by saying, "The boy decided to ask Santa to go to his house with a ball, a book, and a toy train." A more acceptable usage might be: "The boy was bouncing his ball on the train. The conductor told him to go to his seat and sit quietly. He suggested that the boy read a book instead."

When the first player is finished, he refolds his words and puts them back in the container. Now the second player selects five words at random to use in a paragraph. They may be five new words, or some of the first player's words may show up again.

Unless the players are bored with the activity, there is no need to stop after everyone has had a turn. If everyone has contributed ten words, even if there are only two players there are plenty of words to choose from. New words will keep popping up.

Top-Secret Languages

Pig Latin is probably the best-known of childhood's secret languages. For those of you whose childhoods are too far behind you or who flunked Pig Latin 101 at age six, it's spoken as follows:

Start the word with the initial vowel sound, putting the initial consonant sound at the end and following it with "ay."

Basket becomes "*asket-bay*," *girl* is "irl-gay," and *gross* is "oss-gray." If a word begins with a vowel, just say the word and follow it with "way." *I* becomes "I-way"; similarly *eye* becomes "eye-way." And *easy* becomes "easy-way."

Pop quiz! Decode the following sentence:"I-way an-cay eak-spay a-way-arned-day ood-gay ig-Pay atin-Lay." Easy, isn't it?

Ah, but so many kids speak Pig Latin that this "secret" language isn't much of a secret anymore. Can your kids dream up another, newer secret language? There are others, of course, already in existence. In my childhood, some kids spoke secret languages involving interpolating the sounds "op" or "obble" into words. But how much more fun it is to invent your own, brand-new, all-your-own language!

Suggest to your child that she set her creative mind to work on devising a new secret language. The rules are all up to her. If she's not familiar with this concept, first teach her Pig Latin so she gets the general idea. If she doesn't jump on the project, remind her that a new language of her invention will be unknown to her classmates, neighbors, and even teachers unless all-powerful she chooses to teach it to them.

When all else fails, bribery usually works, but don't call it bribery—call it motivation!

And Then She Wrote...

For this exercise you'll need to have at least one book of fiction on hand. You can choose an adults' or kids' book, a novel or a collection of short stories. It's better, though, to pick a book with which your child is *not* familiar.

Pick up the book and read approximately a paragraph aloud. The friend who taught me this game picks a passage at random, though I think it's better to choose with some delibera-tion. Then, it's your child's responsibility to pick up where the book left off. He need have no familiarity with the book, no idea what preceded the passage you've read aloud, no clue as to the identity of the characters. In fact, you may have just read a passage absolutely unpopulated by any people. It may describe the scene on a windswept moor, a chilling frost, the emergence of a crocus, or snow blowing across a bleak plain. He is to pick up where the narrative left off and continue with a passage that could logically follow the selection you just read.

If you're playing this with older kids—teens or particularly literate preteens—you can require that they try to emulate the style of the book's author. But that is not essential to the game and shouldn't even be considered with most kids.

As an optional method of play, the child may act out what follows rather than narrate in the voice of the author (or the voice of a character, if the story is ostensibly told by the protagonist or another character). In this case, the child would speak for each of the characters and can even change voices to emulate different ones if he wants, though this is not at all a requirement. The child's contribution that follows the original passage may be a sentence, a paragraph, or longer. When he stops, you can pick another passage out of the same book, or a different one, and again the child chimes in with a suitable follow-up.

Three Cheers for Our School/Town/Team/Club

Let's have a cheer for creativity—a cheer for your city or town, state, or our country—a cheer your child is going to write. Your child (yes, boys too—historically, boys were cheerleaders before girls ever were) can write a cheer for any institution or entity he wants, though those suggested above seem the likeliest candidates.

Surely he can be more original than the old "Two-four-six-eight" formulation. The cheer can be brief or elaborate. Devising accompanying choreography is optional.

Excuses, Excuses!

Is your child a good procrastinator? Is homework left undone till the last possible moment? Are dishes, bath, room straightening, dog washing, and other chores put off till the ultimate hour—or not done at all? Does he at least have a creative excuse for chores being done late or left undone?

Ask your child to dream up some good, clever, creative excuses for tardiness in completing chores or failure to meet responsibilities. He should be imaginative, and if humor enters into the picture, that's even better. But he shouldn't use those same excuses at a later time for failure to perform real tasks. You can always say, "Uh-uh-uh! I've heard that one already."

Chapter 4

Designs and Inventions

Creativity involves creating *things* as well as words and pictures. The person who writes a computer program, invents a new device, or builds the proverbial new-and-improved mousetrap is being just as creative as the artist, musician, or writer. And while kids can't be expected to design a working robot, they *can* invent games, design new layouts for their bedrooms, and dream up other totally plausible neat stuff.

Set the gears in your child's brain turning in the direction of new inventions, ideas, improvements on existing things, and such. Here are some suggestions for ideas that can be harvested from your child's fertile brain.

Turnabout Is Fair Play

For centuries, teachers have been grading kids on their grasp of math, English, and other subjects. But how good are the teachers? Just what are the aspects of teaching and relating to kids on which teachers should be graded, anyhow? Ask your child to devise a report card that grades teachers on the things your child thinks are important. These might include:

- explains subjects clearly
- is patient
- grades fairly
- doesn't lose his temper
- sets up fair and reasonable rules
- gives reasonable homework
- has reasonable expectations of kids
- is fair in punishment and discipline

Or your child may have her own set of standards on which to grade teachers. She should not only think of categories on which to grade teachers but should lay out the format for the report card and indicate what the marking system is (U/S, A/B/C/D/E/F, 0–100, or some other scheme).

If she's enterprising, and you have a photocopier at home, she might even duplicate the report card and sell copies to friends!

Variations: Along the same line, and in the spirit of Calvin in the comic strip *Calvin and Hobbes*, with his Dad Approval Ratings, your child may want to devise a report card for parents. (Hey—that's you!) She may also think of other people she could write a report card for: summer camp counselors, music or gymnastics teachers, or someone else.

School Daze

A report card might show your child's teachers how they could be better, but how could the whole school building be better? Suppose your child could redesign the school itself? Would he make it one-story so there are no stairs to climb? Or would he make it multi-story so there are fewer, shorter halls to walk? Put the school's library in a more central location for easier access? Have a computer at every child's desk? Or, more fancifully, put a yard complete with plants, picnic benches, and playground equipment on the roof for al fresco lunch and recreation in fair weather? Build a swimming pool in a separate building adjacent to the school, with a retractable dome so swimming is done outdoors in good weather, indoors in bad?

Install a tram or monorail along one side of each hallway so kids who don't want to walk from their classroom to the cafeteria, gym, library, music room, or the principal's office can ride? Have a stable attached to the school so kids can take riding lessons instead of gym? Have conveyor belts alongside every row of desks for passing out papers and collecting homework and tests so nobody has to get up and file to the front of the room? Have small Pizza Hut, Taco Bell, McDonald's, Baskin-Robbins, and other franchises in the cafeteria instead of the usual food? Have a jacuzzi the kids could use as a P.E. activity? Have a zoo or museum right at the school?

Ask your child to sit down and design a school from scratch, one that doesn't need to resemble his present one at all, but that is ideal from his viewpoint. He should create at least two designs: one overhead view of the entire building, or of each floor if it's multi-storied, and one detailed view of the ideal classroom. Would the desks be arranged in rows, in a circle, or clusters? Where would the teachers's desk be? What else would be in the room? He should be detailed and specific. You can suggest that your child's design be realistic and practical, or imaginative and fanciful. You could even suggest that he do two designs, one practical and one fanciful.

Give Me Shelter

While your child is designing buildings, why not have her design the ideal home: Again, the design can be either practical or fanciful, or she can do one of each. Would your child's ideal home have a brook meandering through the living room so she could fish for her dinner without traveling any distance or braving the elements? Would it have a glass roof so she could look up at the stars from her bed until she fell asleep? Would there be an escalator between floors so she wouldn't have to climb stairs? A workout room with full gym equipment?

What about her own room? She surely will want to draw a design for that as well as for the house as a whole. Again, the design can be practical, fanciful, or one of each. If your child is very young, she may put fanciful items in the practical category, leaving it to you to explain why a robot to clean up the room is impossible, a conveyor belt to carry dirty dishes to the kitchen is impractical, a TV screen that takes up the better part of one wall is too darned expensive, and Astroturf on the floor wouldn't work in the long run.

If you live in an apartment building—or an apartment is your child's ideal home—she may want to redesign the whole building, too.

Hop, Skip, and Jump

One of the funnier bits that the comic group Monty Python did involved the Ministry of Silly Walks. Your child too can invent a silly walk. Hop after every two steps? Wiggle your feet along the ground to propel yourself forward? Splay your feet outward as you walk? What other funny means of pedestrian locomotion can your child devise?

This exercise mixes creativity with physical activity, and your child can have a good time practicing different silly walks to see which ones are worth remembering or writing down. Unlike some of the activities in this section that involve sitting and drawing, this one involves the child in an active pursuit while he's thinking.

There's an expression—"thinking on your feet." Though the original meaning is something different, the phrase certainly applies here.

On Your Market, Set, Go

That's how one adult told me, as a child, he heard the starter's warning: "On your market, set, go!" Well, your child can get on his mark, get set, and go off to figure out new kinds of races— relay or otherwise—that she and her friends might run either casually, at an outdoor birthday party, or on a school field trip.

If she can't think of any races, start her motor running by reminding her that there are duckwalk races, wheelbarrow races, walking-backward and side-shuffle races, hopping and skipping races, three-legged races, and races in which the runner has to carry a potato on a spoon, blow at a balloon and keep it in the air as she runs, or perform some other task while running. Now that you've primed her brain, what other types of races can she dream up? Who knows—she may even think up some of the activities for her next birthday party!

Tripping the Light Fantastic

Now that he's thought of silly walks and fun races, how about inventing the next dance craze, or at least one dance step? Well, *somebody* invented everything from the lindy to moshing, and is his invention likely to be any sillier than the swim, or sillier-named than the mashed potato? So let your child dance his heart out, and maybe if he's inventive he'll dream up the next craze to sweep the country—or at least his elementary school.

For your sake, let's hope that it's not a dance that involves a lot of stamping.

I'm Game

I'm game to learn a new game. Are you game for a new game? Good—then let your child invent one. It's not that difficult.

If you set a couple of empty soda cans on a fence and throw rocks at them, that's a pastime. Now regulate rock throwing with a few rules: You have to stand behind the lilac bush to throw. If you knock a can over you get a point. If you can knock it beyond the flat grey rock over there, you get two points. Everybody throws one rock at a time, and the first one to score ten points wins. Now you have more than an idle pastime—you have a game.

If you take a large piece of cardboard and draw squares all around it, you have a rudimentary game board. A paper clip, penny, nail, nut (hardware type or edible), or similar small items can be game pieces. Decide what will determine how many squares each piece moves on each turn. A roll of dice? A spin of a spinner from a boxed game you have at home? Picking a card at random from among an ace, deuce, three, and four? Will some squares have penalties on them? ("Go back three spaces.") Does a player have to answer a question or accomplish a feat in order to move the number of squares determined by the deciding factor? What other rules and outside factors will influence the moves of the playing pieces?

There are board games, other quiet games, active games, games for one, two, or large groups, and there's no reason why your child can't invent one or more games. It may not be commercially salable or earn her millions of dollars in royalties (though somebody certainly invented Scrabble, Monopoly, and Clue), but think of the satisfaction and pride she'll feel sitting down with her friends or family to play the game *she* invented!

Boredom Is the Mother of Invention

The next time your child complains he's bored, there's nothing to do, or even when he's uttered no such complaint, give him an assortment of unrelated items and see what he can do with them. He might create a piece of art, invent a game, or devise a new toy.

Give him some or all of the following: a piece of scrap material, a piece of construction paper, a piece of crepe paper, a stick, a safety pin, scissors, a pen, glue, marking pens, buttons, and marbles. Add other items—you know what you have around the house. While he inventing something he won't be bored, and he may create something he can play with long after he's created it.

Edison the Second

Your child will be in good company if, like Edison, she invents something the world can use. But even if she never sees her invention translated into a practical design she'll have fun thinking about it—and stretching those creative muscles along the way.

If your child is a computer buff, as so many kids are today, you can nourish your child's budding computer genius with this exercise in computer-oriented inventiveness that requires no knowledge of programming. Ask your child to think about the kinds of problems that confront people and the solutions that computers might offer. Then ask, "What sort of computer programs would you write to solve these problems if you could?"

Note that you are not asking your child to actually write the program; all you are asking is that she say, "I would write a program that would make the computer ring a bell at seven thirty every evening, get your attention even if you're not at the computer, and then flash reminder messages for the stuff you need to do to prepare for the next day: Defrost meat for Thursday dinner. Write speech for board meeting. Bake cookies for PTA bake sale. Mail mortgage payment. Write memo to department heads."

Or, "I would write a program to work with a computer's spellchecker that would spot a wrong word that's spelled right, like *were* for *where* or *their* for *there*."

Of course, if your child shows an interest in actually learning to program, you can probably find a class in your city or town that she could take. In time she might even write the program she dreamed up. But even if she doesn't learn to program till she's grown up, that idea will probably still be in the back of her mind. Those ideas stay "filed" in the brain and can take very practical forms years later when the needed knowledge is in place to make the ideas workable. And even if your child's ideas for programs never get translated into practicality, just thinking of ways to improve life through computers—or improve computers themselves—will stretch those creativity muscles.

Chapter 5

Longfellow

Your Child May be a Poet
Even If He Doesn't Know It!

Your child doesn't have to be a famous poet to be comfortable with verse. A little fun fooling around with rhymes will get him into the swing of things poetic, and then he can progress not only to rhymed verse but also to song lyrics, rap songs, and other creative fun with rhythm and rhyme.

Rhyme Time

You can ease your child into poetry gradually by having him rhyme words first. Give your child a word and ask him to think of as many words as he can that rhyme with it. Start with words for which there are many possibilities: *day, be,* and *go* are good choices. If you wish, write a list, of all the words your child can think of that rhyme with each word you suggest. He can refer to the list later when he uses these words to write a simple poem.

If your child enjoys rhyming these words, think of more, again choosing words that are easy to rhyme and offer lots of possibilities. As a general rule, one-syllable words with long vowels in them, such as *late, wheat,* and *ice,* are often good choices.

Writing Simple Poems

Now that your child has had fun with rhyming words, ask her to make up a simple two-line poem using two or more of the rhyming words. For example:

> *Jim thinks that three*
> *Is a nice age to be.*

Or:

> *I like to go*
> *And play in the snow.*

Though these poems are never going to win prizes, your child will have the joy of accomplishment, and once she is comfortable with creating two lines of similar meter that rhyme, she can try writing longer, more sophisticated poetry.

Kids first starting to write poems often try to make *every* line rhyme with the first line. Now would be a good time to explain rhyme schemes to your child, suggesting she write a four-line verse in one of the standard rhyme schemes. When she gets comfortable writing poetry, she can try to formulate a poem in each of the different schemes.

In case you've forgotten, the most common rhyme schemes are AABB, ABAB, ABCB, and ABBA. In the first of these, the first two lines rhyme with each other, and the third and fourth lines rhyme with each other as well. In ABAB the first and third lines rhyme, while the second and fourth lines rhyme. In ABCB only the second and fourth lines rhyme, and in ABBA the first and fourth lines rhyme, while the second and third lines rhyme.

Of course there are other possibilities, including three-line, six-line, and multi-verse poems in which the last line of each verse rhymes with the last line of all the other verses, and various other formulations. If your child wants to explore other forms or lengths, by all means encourage her.

The next step beyond a simple four-line verse, though, is probably going to be a multi-verse poem. If your child can't think of what to write a poem about, here are some suggestions:

- a poem about weather, clouds, seasons, or other aspects of nature
- a poem about a holiday
- a poem briefly retelling a familiar story
- a poem briefly retelling a family story or incident
- a poem briefly retelling a historical event
- a poem about a friend or family member
- a poem about a dog, cat, or other animal
- a funny poem

If she has trouble getting started, provide the first line for her and see what she can come up with in the way of subsequent lines for one or more verses. Here are some first lines to get things going:

The clouds are sailing in the sky.
My dog is friendly, small, and brown.
I really love our family's cat.
My teacher's strict, but she is fair.
The sun is bright. Come out and play.
I have a friend. His name is Jim.
My sister tried to cook one night.
Cinderella had sisters as mean as could be.

Poor Hansel and Gretel got lost in the wood.
Blue is my favorite color of all.
Santa had an elf named Holly.

With a little encouragement, your child will soon be creating longer and better poems. So what if her early efforts are pure doggerel? Do you think Edna St. Vincent Millay started at the top?

There Once Was a Poet Named Paul

What is perhaps the least elegant form of verse may be the one most enjoyed by kids: limericks. You're probably familiar with the basic limerick form, the meter of which often varies slightly:

Dah-DAH-dah-dah-DAH-dah-dah-DAH
Dah-DAH-dah-dah-DAH-dah-dah-DAH
Dah-DAH-dah-dah-DAH
Dah-DAH-dah-dah-DAH
Dah-DAH-dah-dah-DAH-dah-dah-DAH

Though limericks are often known for being bawdy, there are quite a few that aren't and are perfectly suited for kids. One example is:

An epicure dining at Crewe
Found quite a large mouse in the stew.
Cried the waiter, "Don't shout
And wave it about,
Or the rest will be wanting one too."

Suggest that your child write a limerick—or several. If you want, get him started by writing the first line yourself. Some possible first lines are:

There was a young fellow named Paul.
There once was a girl named Marie.
Annette was a pain in the rear.
How happy I am to be me.
I went to a party one day.
My teacher is strict as can be.

After your child writes limericks for the above starting lines, he can write others, starting from scratch.

Fill in the Lines

This one requires a little advance work by you. Select a poem that's likely to catch your child's attention, one with good imagery, catchy rhyme or rhythm, and one that's not beyond his comprehension. It also should be a poem with which he is not already familiar. Copy it on a piece of paper, omitting every other line, but leaving a space in which your child can write.

Present this partial poem to your child and ask him to fill in the blanks—that is, write a line to replace each missing line. Your child should make a reasonable effort to emulate the style of the original writer. His success will depend in part on his age, his command of the English language, and his familiarity with poetry. The finished poem should present a cohesive thought, have a consistent meter and rhyme scheme, and as many lines as the original.

In Training for a Grammy

A child who is older or more advanced in writing rhymed lines can try his or her hand at writing song lyrics. Here the lines need to not only fit the rhyme scheme and meter, they need to fit the music.

What music? Probably a song your child already knows, whether it's a top-ten rock number from the radio, a standard like "On Top of Old Smoky" or "Oh Susanna," a Broadway classic such as "Oh, What a Beautiful Morning," or a kids' song such as "Twinkle, Twinkle Little Star."

Kids in many summer camps across the nation write songs to the tune of well-known songs, and your child can swipe an idea from them for one kind of song to work on. The pep song or comic song you may have sung in camp can be the inspiration for a family song your child can write. Camp pep songs contain many verses, some as brief as only two lines, some longer. Each verse is set to a different tune that is often thematically related to the topic of the pep song verse. For instance, a song about counselors having trouble getting kids out of bed at reveille might be set to the tune of "Oh What a Beautiful Mornin'," "Oh, How I Hate to Get Up in the Morning," or even "Reveille" itself. But the correlation between the topic of the original tune and the topic of the pep song is not essential. I can remember one summer in camp when "Oh, What a Beautiful Mornin'" became "Oh, What a Terrible Laundry." The words fit that tune perfectly, so the tune was appropriated for the verse.

Your child can do the same kind of thing with a family song, writing different verses to different existing tunes. What are some of the family's foibles and funny situations that can be recorded in verses set to music?

• Does Mom's favorite cake recipe inevitably fail?

• Did Fluffy jump up on Mom's visiting boss's lap and frighten the boss into spilling her coffee on the new oriental rug?

• Did Sis wash her new red blouse with the rest of the wash, resulting in Dad's underwear turning pink?

• Did Brother get a new drum set for his birthday, the playing of which has resulted in headaches, or even visits from the police?

• Did the barbecue grill char the steaks to total ruin the night dad's boss was the dinner guest?

• Does Great-Aunt Lucille always call Susan "Marie" when she comes to visit?

• Did little brother set up a lemonade stand, selling the stuff at five dollars a glass in order to make a better profit, then wonder why he didn't have any customers?

These are all suitable topics for verses of the family song, along with any other incidents that may be funny in the retelling—or singing—even if they weren't funny at the time they happened. Besides one-time occurrences, also include any recurring situations that might lend themselves to song. Is little brother creative in his methods for avoiding getting to bed on time? Immortalize that in a verse of the family song—and be sure he's one of the kids who writes the family song, too. Harness that creativity, and hone it!

But a family pep song or comic song is not the only kind your child can write to someone else's music.

• How about a new patriotic song?

• Why not wax patriotic about your home town or community, as well as our country?

• How about an alma mater for your child's school?

Of course, your child can write virtually any kind of lyrics she wants, on any topic at all, and in any style—rock, rap, or whatever appeals to her. If she has an older sibling who plays around with music, maybe the sibling can even write an *original* tune for some lyrics.

Maybe we'll see your child onstage at the Grammy awards in a few years!

Chapter 6

Mixed-Media Creativity

Some projects involve words *and* pictures, or some other combination of media. Many kids are good with words but not pictures, or vice versa. But don't fret—some of the projects in this section involve art but require no artistic talent. And even if a project does require some artistic ability, nobody's judging your child by his abilities—or lack of them. So let your child jump in, have fun, and exercise his creative muscles in the process.

These Balloons Don't Need Helium

Your child can practice being a cartoonist without being able to draw so much as a stick figure! After all, half the trick in comic strips is to get funny words in the characters' mouths.

Your part in all this is to find a comic, either a one-panel strip (such as "The Family Circus") or a multi-panel strip (such as "Peanuts"), and white out or gently erase the dialogue in all the balloons or the caption strip beneath the comic. When the correction fluid has dried, present it to your child and suggest she think of dialogue to write into the balloons or replace the original caption. She doesn't have to draw a thing!

Funny Stuff

Once your child gets the hang of writing the captions for comics, he may feel hampered by being required to work within the framework of someone else's drawings and situations. It's time for him to draw some comics from scratch.

If he isn't much of an artist, he can certainly draw stick figures. If the dialogue doesn't depend on the characters' actions—kicking a ball, eating spinach, or doing something more than just talking—he can even draw talking faces with no bodies. But of course, a comic strip that fully integrates words and pictures is usually preferable, if only because the artist has more options for situational captions. Two characters talking can result in some funny lines, but add a parrot, a plate full of sautéed liver, an Easter egg hidden in the sugar bowl, or Santa peeking in the window and the opportunities for humor are much greater.

Still, if all your child is able to draw is talking heads, he can get a lot of mileage out of that.

Captions Outrageous

Similar to "These Balloons Don't Need Helium" is "Captions Outrageous," an activity that finally finds a use for photos that "didn't quite come out right." And kids with no artistic talent will be pleased that this activity, though involving art, requires no drawing ability whatsoever.

Got a bunch of pictures in your last batch that didn't make the cut? Some may be outright funny on their own: Aunt Cheryl is standing in front of a small, thin maple, and it appears to be growing out of her head. Rover lifted his leg against the car just as the camera went off. Little Roger spilled his ice cream on his shirt just as the shutter clicked.

Others may simply not have made it into the family album because mom was squinting, Caitlin didn't look as good in this one as in the other three, or the exposure was a little off. Nothing really funny there—but there may be by the time your child is through with them.

Take all the rejects you were going to throw out anyway, whether inherently funny or just inadequate for the family album, and give them to your child along with scissors, pen, glue or paste, and white paper. It's up to her to write either below-the-picture captions or dialogue to go in comic-strip style "balloons."

If her captions are to appear below the picture, she can paste a strip of white paper, with the captions written on it, below the photo. Dialogue for balloons should be written small, within an area that would make a suitable-sized balloon. Then the balloon is cut out of the white paper and pasted onto the photo.

The photo of the tree apparently growing out of Aunt Cheryl's head might inspire a balloon from Aunt Cheryl's mouth with the comment, "This is a great climate for growing things," "Have you got any aspirin? I've got an awful headache," or "One advantage is I'll always have shade in the summer." Pictures that aren't as inherently funny may not inspire the same kind of zany captions, but with a little thought, something funny will occur to your child for *some* of the pictures.

Don't make her strain to caption every picture. Some just won't inspire funny comments.

Creature Features

Fantastic monsters or cuddly animals? Your child can decide for himself when you ask him to dream up an original creature, something that doesn't exist in real life. It may be an animal, a resident of another planet, or a humanoid form like the Yeti that lives on Earth but belongs to a shy, never-seen species. It may be friendly, shy, or hostile, beautiful, stark, cuddly, frightening, or simply odd.

Your child may choose to create something that doesn't look like anything you've seen before. Or he may draw a creature that has very recognizable parts that have simply never met on a single being before: the feet of a duck on the legs of a stork, the bill of a pelican below the trunk of an elephant, the hump of a camel, the pocket of a kangaroo, and tiger stripes to cover it all.

Give him paper and crayons (or colored markers) and ask him to create a creature, one that doesn't exist in real life. when the drawing is complete, ask questions. These might include:

- What is the creature called?
- Where does it live?
- What does it eat?
- What kind of sound does it make?
- How big is it?
- Does it have fur, feathers, or scales?
- Does it bear live young or lay eggs?
- Does it have any special abilities?
- What are its other distinguishing characteristics?

Feel free to ask any other questions that occur to you. Other questions may be prompted by specific features of the picture, or the answers your child gives to the earlier questions.

Mixed-Media Homemade Alphabet Book

This is a good project for either a young child just learning her alphabet or a slightly older sibling who feels like being helpful to her younger brother or sister.

For the project, you need to assemble: crayons or markers; paste or glue; scissors; construction paper; a heavy-duty stapler or a hole punch; yarn, fasteners, or a small loose-leaf notebook; and colorful pictures from magazines, photographs you don't want, greeting cards you're not keeping, or any other sources that come to mind.

On each page your child draws one large letter of the alphabet (or two, a capital letter and its lower-case version). Then she hunts for a picture of something that starts with that letter. Cutting the picture out, she pastes it onto the page. Somewhere in the space remaining, she writes the word that pictures represents: "house," "egg," "banana."

If she cannot find a picture for a couple of the more difficult letters, she may have to draw a xylophone or zebra, but with enough resources for pictures—possibly over a period of time, and not all in one day—she should be able to find pictures for most of the letters.

Note that some pictures can be used for more than one letter. For instance, a picture of a woman can be used for *W* (woman) or *P* (person). Cutting the picture up instead of using it whole, your child can get quite a few body parts that are suitable: head, face, arm, leg, and so on. Even these can be broken up into subparts: a picture of an arm can be used whole (arm) or can supply elbow, wrist, shoulder, hand, and fingers.

When each of the twenty-six letters has a page of its own, the book is ready to be fastened together. You can use heavy-duty staples, a hole punch and fasteners, or for greater permanence you can put the whole thing into a small loose-leaf binder, perhaps titling the front with a marker: Linda's own ABC Book.

Picture It Literally

Some expressions, though they have a particular meaning, can conjure up vastly different mental pictures if you disregard (or are oblivious to) the intended meaning. You know what a spelling bee is, but someone who's never heard the expression before might conjure up visions of an insect drawing letters in the dirt with its stinger or sitting at a desk drawing letters with a pen. "Round robin" might induce mental pictures of a fat bird. How about "fencing match"—can you see two matchsticks duelling?

Ask your child to think of expressions that might be similarly misinterpreted, then have him draw pictures depicting the alternate interpretations. You—or your child's friends, brothers, or sisters—can try to guess the expressions he's depicted after he draws them.

Illustrated Family History

Even writing nonfiction offers an opportunity to develop creativity and flair. Your child may groan at the idea of writing biographies if her experience with this form has been solely writing biographical essays for school. Indeed, looking up facts about long-dead historical figures can get pretty dry.

But one nonfiction project your child can get into that won't seem dry or dull is writing a history of the family. This can take the form of writing biographies about immediate relatives: Grandma and Grandpa on both sides of the family, or even Mom and Dad. Or it can take the form of your family's story as far back as it can be traced, but not in the form of a family tree, but rather as an actual story.

Here the "research" doesn't involve looking up facts in library books, but rather asking grandparents, aunts and uncles, cousins, and anyone else in the family for facts about all your ancestors: Who came over from which countries in what year? How old were they then? What were their occupations? Where did they live? Include any other data your child can accumulate. This can involve not just dry facts but human interest stories, family tales about long-gone ancestors, and even "history" of questionable veracity, which your child should identify in her history as a possible myth, or with similar cautionary words.

The history can be illustrated with photographs of the people involved, if photos are available. Pictures of houses where family members lived, relatives' pets, and anything else pertinent would also be appropriate. Your child can also draw whatever pictures she feels are suitable. Finally, the finished product can be typed and placed between two sheets of construction paper to form a "book."

Chapter 7

Miscellaneous Creativity

Not all creativity involves drawing, cutting and pasting, writing, rhyming, or designing and inventing. Some involves mostly thinking. (More on thinking activities in the next chapter.)

Solo Word Treasures

For this solitaire game, your child will need a Scrabble board and tiles. The idea is for her to make as many words as she can by herself. Depending on her age and proficiency with words, she can proceed according to any one of these sets of rules:

• Place all the tiles upside-down and then draw ten of them. Make one word at a time. Replace used tiles with fresh ones. Score according to standard Scrabble scoring. When you have used all the tiles or as many as you can, the game is over.

• Place all the tiles upside down and then draw ten of them. Disregard the scoring patterns on the board; instead give yourself one point for every word of five letters or fewer, two points for a six- or seven-letter word, four points for an eight-letter word, and seven points for any word of nine or more letters. If you add letters to existing words to make new words, you get credit for the whole word if it is not an -ing, -ed, -er, -s or -es ending that you are adding. For example, you have "scream" on the board. You cannot add "er" to claim credit for an eight-letter word. But if you have "make" and add "shift" to it, you can claim credit for "makeshift," a nine-letter word. As above, replace used tiles with fresh tiles. When you have used all the tiles, or as many as you can, the game is over.

• Spread out all the tiles face-up from the beginning. Make the most and longest words you can think of, scoring according to the rules in the variation above.

All the World Loves a Clown

For most kids, the best part of the circus is the clowns. Little kids frequently believe clowns are born with big red noses, orange hair, bright orange circles on their cheeks, and even large shoes—which surely contain equally large feet. As they grow older, kids learn that clowns are really ordinary people who simply put on outrageous clothes and makeup, develop silly routines, and amuse the audience with their antics. The magic is gone but the enjoyment remains.

Your child can be a clown too. He may never join Ringling Brothers, but using your lipstick, blush, eye liner, and even eye shadow he can perfect a style of clown makeup, get together a raggedy or funny outfit, and practice some kind of routine, whether it's pantomine, juggling, or some sort of physical comedy.

Make 'em laugh!

Props

The game of Props is more than a creativity-enhancer—it's good, old-fashioned, laugh-out-loud fun for one child with one parent watching or a whole bunch of kids with visiting parents playing along. In other words, you only need one person to play, but you really want at least one other person to watch, or to play. On the other hand, it's also great for a houseful of kids at a birthday party or other gathering. Why not stretch your child's friends' creativity too!

Start by assembling an assortment of props. Anything around the house will do: a yardstick, magnet, horseshoe, salt shaker, piece of paper, screwdriver, spoon, hula hoop, TV remote control, broom, grater, lampshade, empty wastebasket—you get the idea.

If only one child is playing, hand him the first prop and let his imagination run wild. All he's expected to do is use the prop in as many creative "bits" as he can dream up.

If you hand your son a broom, he might hold it out in the manner of a conductor holding a baton and pretend to lead an orchestra. Then, twirling it, he might pretend to be a drum major. A minute later, the broom becomes a gun he's shooting, and immediately thereafter it's the gearshift lever in a car. He continues in this manner till he runs out of ideas.

Now hand him another prop, say a pencil. In quick succession, this might become a unicorn horn, a drumstick, a lollipop, a rocket lifting off its launching pad, an arrow, a singer's microphone, a cigar....When he runs out of ideas it's time for another prop.

But don't be too quick to yank one prop away and hand the child another. While the child is likely to move from one idea to another at a relatively quick pace, slowing down does not necessarily indicate a total cessation of ideas. Give the child a chance to think. Only if he gives up, or if it seems he's really stumped, should you change props.

With two or more kids playing, you can sit them all in a circle and pass one prop around, letting each child take a turn and pass the prop on. The kids take as many turns as they want till no one can think of any more bits to do. Then start passing another prop from child to child, or give each child one prop to hold and utilize in turn.

After each child has had one turn with a prop, everyone passes his prop to the child on his left, and everyone takes a turn doing a bit with the new one. Keep passing the props around till every child has had every prop at least once, but more often, if they can think of additional bits to do with some of the props.

The bits can be as brief as simulating a baton, or they can be somewhat more complex. They can be silent, as in the example above, or they can involve dialogue, as with the child who brandishes a TV remote control and says, "Set phasers on 'Stun'." They can involve another person, as with the child who puts a pen between another person's lips, removes it, and says, "You're running quite a fever, Mr. Robbins."

Prop players can easily become prop addicts, rummaging in the basement or attic to find suitable props, exhorting you not to dispose of that three-legged chair, those old bike handlebars, that paintbrush or set of old rusted curtain rings. You know how easy it is for an addict to get hooked. How nice it would be to have your child hooked on a creative form of fun.

New-Style Fortunes

For generations, kids have been telling other kids' fortunes by way of a device called a fortune-teller, which is made of folded paper. But here's a new system! As with old-style fortune-tellers, it involves writing the fortunes in advance (which is where the creativity comes in).

Your child will need a pen, perhaps four or six sheets of paper, one die, and, optionally, as many crayons of different colors as sheets of paper. Here's how she proceeds:

At the top of each sheet of paper, write the name of a color with a pen or, preferably, a crayon of that color. For example, if you have five sheets of paper, they could be labelled "orange," "green," "violet," "yellow," "blue," and "maroon." Fold each sheet of paper in half and write the name of the color again somewhere on the outside of the sheet. Unfold the sheets and dream up six brief fortunes per color. Write them down on the inside of each sheet, numbering them one through six. Here are examples:

1. You will marry someone very rich.
2. You will be president of a huge corporation.
3. You will have seven kids.
4. You will be vice president of the United States.
5. You will live to be 120.
6. You will be a teacher.
7. Your daughter will be a famous ballerina.

You need six for each color, and though it is all right to repeat a few of the fortunes, you should try to use new ones on every sheet.

To tell someone's fortune, first show him the *outside* of the sheets so he can see the colors but not the fortunes. Ask him to pick a color from among those on the sheets. Then ask him to roll the die. Now read the corresponding fortune on the appropriate color sheet.

A Wish List for the World

Sometimes daydreaming can lead to practical achievements. This activity starts as an exercise in pure daydreaming, but it can sometimes lead to more concrete accomplishments.

Ask your child to write a wish list for the world. If he doesn't want to write it down, just ask him to tell you his wish list. It will probably contain wishes for peace, no hunger, and no parents hurting or being mean to their kids. Little kids may come up with simplistic entries such as "No bad guys." Older kids will come up with some very adult wishes.

When your child is out of ideas, ask him to think of ways that his wish list might actually be accomplished. What steps can people take right now to bring about the situations your child would wish for? And what, specifically, can your child or his friends do to bring them about?

To promote world understanding and peace he could correspond with a pen pal in another country. To create a "greener" Earth he could clean up trash from the roadside. Even the longest journey begins with a single step.

A Drive Through the Imagination

This activity begins in the realm of the familiar, but it quickly moves into the realm of the imagination. It begins with a drive in a car, and in fact, it can even be played in a car. This possibility makes it a valuable game for parents who want to occupy their child on a boring car trip when the cry of "Mommy, aren't we there yet?" seems to echo from the back seat as regularly as a Swiss cuckoo. This game will not only take up some of the time but do so creatively.

This activity works just as well in the living room, at the dinner table, during a ten-minute settling-into-bed time—whenever. It requires no props or material, just the child's memory and imagination.

You get the game going with a question to your child along the lines of: "You know the way to Davy's house? You go along the shady road past the school, turn left by the big red house with the willow tree in the front yard. And then...." You continue describing the route, watching for the familiar gleam in your child's eye that shows that he's following you, seeing the road in his mind, following the route to Davy's house.

"You know where you turn into Davy's driveway?" you continue. "Well, suppose instead of turning in you kept going straight. What do you think you might see along the road?" If your child knows where that road goes, pick either a different destination than Davy's house or a different route upon deviating from the familiar turnoff point, turning along the next street beyond Davy's, or in some way striking out on a different path from the familiar and known. Of course, if your child knows the whole town pretty well, he's too old or knowledgeable for this game.

But to get back to—if Robert Frost will pardon us—the road not usually taken, once you have mentally guided your child to Davy's driveway and than directed him to keep going into uncharted territory, there are several ways he can carry out the exercise. All are good in their own ways.

He may run off in a flight of fancy. "I think there's a field with elephants grazing in it. Yes, elephants, with ballerinas dancing on their backs. Ballerinas in pink tutus. And a ringmaster." This child has the circus on his mind. Unless he is very, very young, he probably knows that there are not really elephants in the field beyond Davy's house—if indeed there is even a field—but he is having fun imagining.

On the other hand, he may use logic. Logic requires creativity too, although a different type, and the logical answer is just as valuable and valid as the flight-of-fancy answer. The logical child may reason: If Davy lives on a block of two-story brick houses there are probably more two-story brick houses on the next block. And in all of those houses there are probably lots of kids, so maybe there's a school. And maybe a supermarket. And a library. His answer, then, will run along those lines, indicating a good grasp of how neighborhoods are put together.

Or—especially if he's older—he may reason along the lines

of, "I hear the fire whistle coming from that direction, so I bet the firehouse is beyond Davy's house. And his mom walks to work, so probably there's an office building there. And Davy's brother walks to the ballfield, so maybe that's beyond Davy's house. And if those things are there, then there's probably not many more houses. Maybe there's more offices. Maybe there's stores, like near Daddy's office. Maybe tall buildings. Maybe even a train station. I hear a train from somewhere in that direction."

The parent can also ask the child to dream up an adventure that occurs while he's riding along the road beyond Davy's. The exercise will go far beyond "What do you suppose is along that road?" Encourage it.

The other extreme is a child who says, "How should I know what's beyond Davy's house?" This is a child whose creativity muscles are in dire need of stretching. You have two ways to approach him. Either way, encourage his imagination by asking him to flat-out pretend, letting his fancy run free.

You might suggest a possible scenario—the field of elephants above, or some other equally unlikely sight. Then say, "What do you think might be there?" Or you can appeal to logic: "What do you think is probably there? Do you think there's a railroad track? A lake full of swans? How about a factory? A church? Do you think there's frog pond? What about a used car lot? A high school?" The child will be called upon to use knowledge he already has to creatively draw a logical conclusion.

• He knows what's on the street leading up to Davy's.

• He knows that most neighborhoods don't change abruptly, with really nice houses right next door to factories, or run-down apartment houses next to elegant stores.

• He knows that, as a rule, changes in neighborhoods' contents and character come about gradually.

So he can surmise that, whatever the character of Davy's

neighborhood, it probably continues unabated for at least a moderate distance. If Davy lives in a neighborhood of houses with lush lawns, there's probably more of the same for a while, possibly with a school, library, church, or synagogue interspersed.

It might be fun sometime—after he's guessed the character of the road beyond Davy's driveway—to take him for a drive out that way, to let him see just what is along the road in that direction.

Who Lives in That House?

You can go two directions with this activity. One will exercise your child's logical reasoning; the other will stretch her imagination. Either way, you start by pointing out a house your child is not familiar with. Ask your child, "Who do you suppose lives in that house?"

At that point, if you seek a logical answer, your child looks for clues: A toy in the yard indicates the presence of at least one child. A tricycle and a bike indicate that there are at least two kids. A doll probably means there's a girl there; a football means it's a good chance there's a boy. Roses? Someone who cares about gardening. An old car in mint condition? A person who's into vintage cars, more likely male than female.

Is the yard a mess? Possibly whoever lives there is a sloppy housekeeper. Is the house itself in decrepit shape? What does your child think that indicates about the occupants? Is it a large house? A tiny one? What might the size say about the number of occupants? Is there a tall hedge? Are the blinds drawn? What else is distinctive about the house or the grounds surrounding it? What does each of these features suggest to your child?

On the other hand, your child can decide who lives there based on nothing but pure imagination. The Prince of Wales, a frog prince, a navy frogman, a member of the Swiss navy, a manufacturer of Swiss cheese? His teacher's mother? Old Mother Hubbard? The dogcatcher?

Even if your child's decision as to who lives in the house is based on an absolute flight of fancy, items visible on and around the house can provide ideas. Chocolate-brown shutters might suggest the resident is a candymaker. A fat chimney might suggest lots of kids—Santa needs to carry lots of toys down it every year. Lots of windows might suggest an older person who doesn't get out much anymore but loves to watch the world go by.

On the other hand, even if your child's decision as to who lives in that house is sensibly based on serious clues, she can make up a story about the occupants after deciding who they are. The story can be about the residents' current life, or it can deal with an incident in their past—whatever pops into your child's head.

Control Panels

How great it would be if we could turn a knob, twist a dial, and control the people and events around us! Suppose a child could tune out a teacher as easily as he changes TV channels! What if he could turn on a friendship with Lee, who's been ignoring his efforts at friendship all semester? Imagine if he could dial in an ability to speak flawless Spanish, or turn off his temper (or Dad's) with a twist of a button!

If your child could design a control panel, that gave him dominion over circumstances not usually under his control, what would it look like? What would it regulate? Would it be an on/off switch to cut off Uncle Harry's teasing? A sliding lever to lower Dad's voice when he starts yelling?

Offer your child several large sheets of paper and some crayons or markers—or for a one-colored control panel just a pen—and suggest he design as many control panels as he'd like.

Won't it be fun for him to control that which he has little or no control over in life, but would like to, if only in his imagination?

Common Denominators

For this activity you'll want to assemble trios of distinct items that have something in common. (If trios aren't possible, pairs will have to do.) Ask your child to find the common denominator. For instance, gather together a butter knife, a screwdriver, and a crowbar. Then ask your child what they all have in common.

There are a number of possible, and valid, answers. All are long and thin in shape. All are metal. All can be used to pry things open. Each has a sharp enough edge that it could damage wood or flesh. If your child is unsure of some answers, she can certainly check them out. Will a magnet stick to all these things? Get one and find out.

In the course of this activity, some new ways of thinking about familiar objects may occur to you or your child. For instance, what do a toothbrush, a pencil, and a staple gun have in common? One good answer is that each requires only one hand to use. A bicycle, a pendant, and a black leather jacket? Each has a chain.

As I said above, it's also possible, but less challenging, to do this exercise with only two items at a time. It's also possible to do this exercise with items you mention but don't display (for example, a large clock downtown with which your child is familiar, a machine she's seen when visiting Grandma's office, or a picture in Aunt Vikki's house). But this requires good visualization—a different skill—and if your child isn't good at visualizing, or isn't that well acquainted with the items in question, she won't see them clearly in her mind and may not be able to come up with good answers as readily.

"I Can Fly"

So says your child, and now he's going to tell you all about it. For this activity he needs to imagine he's a bird—but first he needs to decide exactly what kind of bird he is. Then ask him to describe flight, the flapping and soaring. There's more to flying than just "I move my wings and go through the sky," and you want to encourage your child to imagine all the details, then relate them to you.

There's pushing off the ledges of buildings, catching the wind and soaring on the draft without effort, swooping down on fish in the sea (if he's chosen to be a pelican, for instance), or flying down to peck for worms in the ground (like a sparrow, among others) or bugs in the wood of trees (a woodpecker). How does it feel to land? To clutch a branch with your feet to keep from falling off? To follow the leader in a formation of birds migrating north or south? How does the bird feeder in your backyard look to a cardinal approaching it from above? How does a crow feel upon realizing it's landed on a scarecrow?

There's far more to flying than just flapping your wings. Realizing this may make your child aware that there's far more to many activities than meets the eye—and that thinking about various activities and their components is worthwhile, as well as good exercise for the mind.

Your child now thinks he knows what it's like to be a cardinal. How is it different from being a pelican? A snow goose? A mallard? An osprey? An ostrich?

Hello, Dolly

Your child probably already uses dolls for creative play. Whether your child is a girl, with the ubiquitous Barbies, or a boy, with "action figures" (don't call them dolls to your son's face!), he probably already uses them in various scenarios.

Most of the time the dolls are probably in character. Your daughter, playing with Barbies, probably invents dialogue for them that's appropriate to Barbie and her friends. Your son, with his action figures, probably has them mostly in war situations, basic training, or other military or rescue situations. But what if you suggested that Barbie, Ken, G.I. Joe, and the others are actors, and that they play parts?

If your child is at all interested in rock or rap musicians, movie or TV stars, suggest that Barbie, Ken, G.I. Joe, and the others play the parts of these stars, and perhaps the parts of other people involved with them—fans, an agent, a producer, a movie or recording executive, or whoever else your child feels is suitable.

Your child can even create props for the dolls: For instance, electric guitars can be cut out of cardboard; shoeboxes can be used as amplifiers. Other scenarios are possible for doll play. You might suggest, "Why not play that your dolls are kids in line at Disney World?" or "How about pretending they're all on board the space shuttle?" or "Next they could all be explorers at the South Pole."

Merely dressing dolls up isn't awfully creative, but playing a game with them, complete with inventing dialogue, stretches those creativity muscles very nicely.

Make It Float

This is an exercise in a scientific brand of creativity. The goal is suggested in the title—trying to see if various items float and experimenting with means of making them float if they don't do so at first.

For instance, your child might take an empty milk container, rinse it out, and put it in a sinkful of water to see if it floats. Or he might cut the bottom off it (if he's too young to use a knife he needs to ask you to do the cutting). Now…will the cut-off bottom float without all that air in the intact container making it buoyant?

Corks float. Bricks don't. He probably already knows this; if not, now's as good a time as any to find out. But if he uses duct tape to attach four corks to the corners of a brick, now will the brick float? Will a boat-shaped object created out of notebook paper float? Or is being shaped like a boat not enough to make an object float?

With young kids you'll want to keep an eye on the proceedings to make sure they don't try to float rare first editions from your library, every last marshmallow you bought for tonight's sweet potato casserole, or that new beaded silk dress you just bought for the upcoming shindig.

No School Today

For harried moms studying the school calendar and its proliferation of holidays, teacher planning days, and other no-school days, it would seem the last thing we need is *another* day off school. But kids and teachers would universally applaud another holiday popping up in the school year.

For that matter, others outside the school sphere might appreciate a new holiday. If it were a general holiday for which most businesses were closed, employees across the nation would rejoice. Also, any excuse for sales and increased shopping would be welcome to our country's merchants. Then there are the airlines, hotels, and others who benefit from people traveling over a three-day weekend.

What new holidays might your child like to see proclaimed by the Chief Executive and added to the national calendar? More is needed here than just the name of a holiday. Pose the following questions and challenges to your child for each holiday she proposes:

- What is the name of the holiday?
- What or whom does it commemorate?
- When should it be held?
- How should it be celebrated?
- If it's a holiday when sending greeting cards is suitable, design one or more.
- What sort of food might traditionally be eaten on this holiday?
- What other traditions might grow around it?

Sail on, Sail on, Sail on and on

Remember those famous words of Columbus—at least according to the poem we all learned in school? He did sail on, not turning back as the crew wanted, and at the end of his journey was rewarded by discovering a new continent.

Suppose that, in this century, it were still possible to discover a new continent? All right, would you believe an island? Suppose your child were the one to discover that continent or island? What would your young explorer name her discovery? What language would the inhabitants speak? What would they look like? How would they dress? What animals would be native to the continent? What flowers and trees, vegetables, and other plant life would grow there? What would the people native to the continent eat? What would their customs be like?

Those are precisely the questions to pose to your child, inviting her to answer them not only in words but in pictures. Being imaginative as she wants, she should draw and describe the inhabitants' costumes, the continent's plant and animal life, its national holidays and celebrations, and all the other factors that make up this newly discovered civilization. Does it have a flag? How would you translate its national anthem? Its Pledge of

Allegiance? What are some of its local laws? This has the potential for a full-scale fantasy project if your child wants to really run with it.

Five-Four-Three-Two-One

Roger, Houston, we have ignition. Your young space traveler is ready to blast off—at least in her imagination—in the cockpit of a homemade spacecraft that will encourage hours of imaginative play. But first your explorer needs to design the cockpit, and that too takes creativity.

Though boys are still more enamored of rocket ships than girls, we've had female astronauts, and the *Star Wars* audiences certainly numbered many girls among the enthusiastic viewers. So this is by no means an activity for boys only.

Your child's first challenge is to design and build the cockpit, which requires a large carton, probably from a refrigerator, stove, or something of similar size. If you haven't recently taken possession of a giant TV or new deep freezer, visit your local appliance store.

What else can your child utilize in creating the cockpit? That will depend in part on her imagination, and in part on what you have around the house or workshop that you don't mind parting with. Odd knobs and wheels, old dials and gauges, toggle switches, levers, clock faces, and more can be utilized as instruments and controls for the cockpit.

A great basis for a control panel is the styrofoam block material used to pack electronic equipment or kitchen appliances. It can be used as is, carved, or sawed to a smaller size or different shape. It can even be spray painted silver or black for added realism. But lacking styrofoam, your child can attach the controls and gauges directly to the cardboard or she can feel free to create her control panel from something else entirely. These are only suggestions, not requirements.

Remove the legs of a discarded kitchen chair for a realistic-looking pilot's chair—or leave the legs in place and let the child use her imagination even more. Provide two chairs, and your child can have a friend be the copilot or navigator.

Your child can even create a greater appearance of realism by cutting portholes out of the cardboard and inserting black construction paper on which she has drawn stars, moons, or planets in those spaces, or fashion the stars out of silver glitter. Now when she looks out the porthole, she'll see space. True, the scenery won't move to give the appearance of the spaceship being in motion, but that's one more reason for your child's imagination to be called into play.

She can leave the box intact and crawl into it to play inside (and at first to build it), or cut one side out for easier access. Which choice she makes will depend on the carton's size, your child's size, and the strength of her imagination. What levers and controls she installs will depend on what you have lying around and on what her concept of a spaceship cockpit is. Of course, if you have absolutely no dials, levers, gauges, and such lying around the house, the old standby of drawing the controls with a marker is always available, but it hasn't the same degree of realism—or fun.

Your child can opt to be an astronaut from this country and year on an exploration to the moon. Or she can be the captain of a fleet of star cruisers from the year 2155, an explorer from a distant planet, or the pilot of a regularly scheduled shuttle to a space station or the moon. Just make sure your space traveler doesn't go so far beyond Pluto that she can't get back in time for dinner!

One serious note: Children sometimes grasp partial facts and don't realize they don't have the whole picture. I have heard of one case of a child, playing spaceship in a cardboard carton, who set fire to its bottom. Having seen pictures of spacecraft with flames blazing below them, he believed they were set afire to make them take off. Therefore, he believed his own mock spaceship would take off if the bottom were lit. Parents, be cautious.

The Unexpected Guest

What's Kristi Yamaguchi, Mickey Mouse, Aunt Julie, or your child's teacher doing in your guest room? That's for your child to decide in this game that's part flight of fancy, part imagination-stretcher, part exercise in writing dialogue aloud.

First your child has to decide who the unexpected guest is. It might be a real friend or relative, who could plausibly occupy the room, but it's more challenging (and more fun) when the guest is someone unlikely, such as Dan Marino, or impossible, such as Heidi, who's fictional, or Dr. Seuss, who's no longer on this earth.

When your child has decided who is in the guest room (or guest bed), he next has to decide why the guest is there. How did it happen that Darth Vader wound up snoring on your convertible sofa or four-poster bed? What chain of circumstances led him here? It's up to your child to devise a quasi-believable chain of events that led to his sleeping in your guest bed.

Fast-forward to breakfast: What's the conversation across the corn flakes likely to consist of? Ask your child to construct a possible dialogue involving the child and the guest. If he wishes, he may also interpolate conversation from other family members, but a three-part dialogue is too much to ask of many small kids.

As is true of many activities that exercise creativity muscles, this one calls for several different kinds of inventiveness, and an older child can be asked to construct believable dialogue. If you think his dialogue for the guest doesn't sound credible you can

challenge him, "Do you really think that's the way Mark Twain would have talked?" or "Would Donald Duck really say that?"
Variations:

• You decide who the guest is, then leave it up to the child to carry it from there.

• For an older child, when the child explains why the guest is in your guest room, pin him down for a more specific or plausible reason. If the child says Aladdin is in your guest room because he was on his way to Hollywood to make another movie and needed a place to spend the night, ask why he picked your house to visit, or where he was coming from and what he was doing there, or what he was doing in your town if he was on his way from Arabia to Hollywood, or even what the new movie is about.

• For an older child, have him imagine two guests, preferably unrelated (not Bugs Bunny and Elmer Fudd, but rather Tom Sawyer and the President of the United States, or Patrick Ewing and Santa Claus). Now he has to imagine what circumstances caused each of these people to land at your doorstep, and he has to construct a three-part (or more) breakfast dialogue involving both of the guests, the child, and, if he wants, any other family members.

Buck's Big Adventure

Buck, in this activity, is the family dog. If your family's dog is named Duchess or Harrington, or if your family's pet is not a dog but a cat or rabbit, substitute the appropriate name. If allergies, a strict landlord, or other circumstances dictate that your family is petless, substitute your neighbor's dog, your sister's cat, or some other familiar animal.

Your child is going to imagine Buck's big adventure, which can take either of two forms. One is a plausible adventure, such as straying down the street, getting lost, and getting taken in by another family or being turned in to the pound, or (less likely but still within the realm of believability) getting somehow locked into the zoo or local WalMart for the night. Or perhaps appearing on *Letterman* doing Stupid Pet Tricks, or being awarded a medal by the President for somehow courageously saving a small child's or a visiting senator's life. The other is a purely fantastic adventure, perhaps involving a trip to the moon, or a flight across the United States while wearing a jetpack.

Ideally, you'd like your child to imagine some of both kinds of adventures—plausible or at least semi-plausible and pure fantasy. The plausible adventure might involve tangling with a bear in the woods, nearly being hit by a car, or being hit, but then saved by a dedicated vet. In the fantastic adventure the dog could suddenly learn to talk, or he could own a shiny red convertible and know how to drive it.

In either case, in order to create an animal adventure story, your child must put herself in Buck's place, imagining that she's a dog, cat, or rabbit.

If your child has trouble getting a story going, you can set up the circumstances, then have the child take over: "Suppose Buck went with us to Disneyland and somehow got separated from us." "Imagine Buck could talk and went on TV to show off. What do you suppose Oprah or Jay would ask him? What do you suppose he would say about us?"

Shrinking Powder

When I was a kid, one of the comic books I frequently bought featured, as an additional story toward the back of the magazine, the adventures of a girl named Mary Jane who, by reciting a magic verse and wishing, could make herself the same size as a mouse named Sniffles.

Kids have long been fascinated with growing and shrinking,

and what fun it would be if they could do either at will. Ask your child to imagine he had a magic potion that, when swallowed, would shrink him to any size he wanted, or that he had a jar of shrinking powder that would reduce him to the size of a dog, mouse, ant, or any other size he desired when sprinkled on him.

First ask him where he might like to go and what he might like to do if he could shrink at will. Then, when he has spun out his own fantastic voyage, suggest a few scenarios and ask him to pick up from the point at which you left off.

Suggested scenarios:

• Small as a mouse, he scoots through a mousehole to the other side. What does he find? What does he do?

• The size of an ant, he stows away on a spacecraft.

• The head of the FBI has a special assignment for your child because of his ability to shrink himself.

Let's try another angle of questions.

• Word gets out that he has this potion or shrinking powder. Who'd want to get their hands on it?

• What particular uses could people put it to—good *and* bad?

• What would he do when people wanted to buy it from him—or steal it? Would he sell it? Give it away to deserving people? If so, how would he decide who was deserving? Would he hire a security guard to guard it?

Carry the fantasy in yet another direction. Suppose he had the opposite of shrinking powder—a substance that, when splashed on, sprinkled on, or swallowed, makes him grow much bigger.

• What fun could he have with it?

• What good uses could the world put it to?

• What adventures could he have with it?

- Would he share it with friends? The government? Anyone?
- What kinds of work could he get as a direct result of being gigantic? (For example, chopping off the tops of tall trees that are interfering with electric wires, washing second-story windows without a ladder, working on phone poles without climbing them.)
- What problems would he have, specifically due to his size, now that he was 11 or 20 feet tall, or taller?
- What would be the antidote—that is, when your child had had enough of being 10, 20, or 30 feet tall, how would he shrink back to normal?

Finally, for now, ask your child:

- Besides a powder, potion, or lotion for growing and shrinking, what else might you like in the way of magic preparations? (Examples might include "invisible cream"—rub it on and you're invisible. Or a substance that, when swallowed, would give you the power to see for miles or hear what's being said at a great distance. Or the ability to pick up radio stations in your head without a radio.)
- How could people use such powers for their own good?
- How could people use such powers for the good of the world in general?
- How could people misuse such powers and cause harm?

Time Travel

For this exercise of your child's imagination, she needs to start by imagining that staple of childhood fantasies, a time machine. In it she can transport either herself back to another era or real or fictitious people from another era into your living room of today. It doesn't matter which version she does first, but she should try both.

Now ask such questions as:

• What five things in our house do you think Huck Finn would find most fascinating? Why?

• Imagine you're taking George Washington on a tour around our city. What sights do you think would most interest a visiting former President? Next take him on a tour of the country. What do you think he'd say when he saw what the country looks like today?

• If Cinderella were eating dinner with us, what would she find unfamiliar?

• When you put him back in the time machine, what ten things might Davy Crockett want to take with him to make his life easier or more interesting?

Now ask:

• Suppose you're in the time machine. What year should I set it on?

• What are the major differences between that year and this one?

• What ten inventions would you take with you to show the people what life in this era is like? But would a microwave oven work—had electricity been discovered yet?

• Who would you most like to meet if you were traveling back in time?

• What year or era in the past do you think it might have been fun to live in?

• In what way were things better then?

• In what way were things not as good then?

Another line of questions:

• Suppose you could warn people in the past about things that were going to happen. What year should I send you back to first?

• If the people knew that in advance, what do you think they would have done about it?

• What difference would that have made in the course of history?

When Mom and Dad Were Kids...

Kids love to hear tales of their parents' and grandparents' childhoods, and often they're amazed by some of the details. ("You mean you didn't have video games? You didn't have a VCR? You didn't have MTV? What did you *do?*") What kids imagine their parents' childhoods to have been like is often very far from the truth, though sometimes kids' suppositions are surprisingly on target.

The dad who's a strict rule-enforcer now may have been a hell-raiser at ten. The mom who is a capable executive at work and also manages a household flawlessly may have been a totally inept and awkward teen. The parent who regularly gives speeches all across the country may have been tongue-tied, shy, or a stutterer at four or eight.

Here are some questions you can ask your child:

• What sort of a life do you suppose Mom or Dad had as a child?

• What sort of trouble do you suppose Mom or Dad got into when young?

• What sort of adventures do you suppose Mom or Dad had?

• For what infractions do you suppose Mom or Dad got punished?

• What do you suppose the punishments consisted of?

• Were Grandma and Grandpa strict or lenient?

• What do you suppose was the biggest adventure of Mom's or Dad's childhood?

• What do you suppose was the best or most exciting thing that ever happened to Mom or Dad?

• What do you suppose was the worst thing Mom or Dad ever did?

• What was Mom or Dad's favorite place to play?

It's certainly valuable to give your child the actual answers to these questions, but only after asking your child to come up with a creative answer first. Then tell him what your biggest adventure or worst misbehavior consisted of. It's good for children to see their parents as real people, and these little insights help focus that perception.

Secondhand Speculations and First-Rate Creativity

The only material required for this exercise is whatever's found in the nearest antique store, secondhand store, thrift shop, or consignment shop. And you don't even have to buy any of the items in question. Just browse with your child, and ask questions.

Specifically, all the questions run along the lines of, "Tell me about the person who used to own this," or variations on that theme. Your child's imagination can run wild with this question, but you should expect a certain amount of logical deduction too.

If the item is a six-inch-wide tie decorated with psychedelic flowers, it's a pretty safe bet that it belonged to a man in the sixties—not *his* sixties, the *era* of the sixties. In fact, he was most likely in his teens, twenties, or thirties. He may have had long hair, and perhaps wore an earring. His favorite rock group could have been the Beatles. Now we're guessing, just as your child can guess at further details about the tie's owner, letting her imagination run as wild as she wants and making up as many details about the man as she wishes.

Now look around the store and find some other articles for your child. How about a *Happy Days* lunchbox—what can your child deduce about its original owner? And what would she like to further guess about that person? How about a moss-green recliner with hair oil stains on it? A silver serving platter with a long, thin gouge in it? An LP containing Shakespearean passages read aloud? A Tinkertoy set?

What about a paperback jokebook with the back cover missing, and "To L—Use it successfully! Love—M" written in ink inside the front cover? Does the inscription provide a clue? Suppose, instead, the inscription was "Get well quick!" or "Happy Special Birthday—and many more." What might your child conclude then?

Your child will learn to use a certain amount of Sherlockian reasoning. Is it likely that the original owner of the 16-pound bowling ball with silver-dollar-sized fingerholes was a tiny-framed teacher named Ms. Morris? Why not? What do the claw marks on that chair's legs probably indicate? Does the Lego piece behind a sofa's cushion tell your child something?

On the drive or walk home, ask your child to make up a little story about the presumed owner of one of the items she speculated about in the store. If you've asked your child to make up an awful lot of stories lately and suspect she's tiring of that activity, ask her to simply invent a day's schedule for the owner of the red coat with the black mink collar. Or to speculate on what other furnishings and decorations might have been in the same room as the Mickey Mouse telephone. Or what photos might have been taken with the first few rolls of film loaded into the camera your child already decided was once the property of another child. Or why the owner of the purple-flowered lamp no longer owns it. Secondhand speculation can lead to some first-rate creativity!

Chapter 8

Thinking Exercises

Thinking exercises are just what the name implies—questions for your child to think about, questions that seek creative answers, imaginative answers, answers that stretch those mental muscles. Thinking exercises can be indulged in at special times you set aside, intervals of ten minutes or half an hour devoted just to creative and imaginative thinking. Or they can be a means of occupying what would otherwise be boring intervals—during car rides, waiting in line in the supermarket, sitting in the dentist's waiting room, or those ten minutes when homework is finished and dinner isn't quite ready yet.

Thinking exercises work at any age—including yours. Of course not every thinking exercise is suited to every age, but read the questions below and choose the ones best suited to your child. And don't be shy about devising questions of your own!

• Describe a perfect day.

• If you could live anywhere on earth, where would you choose to live, and why?

• If you could live in any kind of house—including not only houses and apartments but tents, igloos, converted barns, or other less-ordinary structures—where would you choose to live? What would it be like?

• What would you like to do that you're not physically able to do now?

• What would you most like to do that you're not permitted to do now?

• If you could be anyone else, who would you choose to be?

• If there were no school to go to, what would you do right now with your life if you could do anything at all?

• If you could have any real person, of any age, as a sister or brother, who would you pick, and why?

• If you could have any fictional person, of any age, as a sister or brother, who would you pick, and why?

• If you could have any famous people as parents, who would you pick, and why?

• If you could have any fictional people as parents, who would you pick, and why?

• Too many dogs are named Spot, King, Rover, and Fido. Think of more inventive, imaginative names for dogs.

• Think of good names for: cats, birds, fish, snakes, hamsters, gerbils, and guinea pigs.

• What about kids? Do they deserve distinctive names too? Or is it a disadvantage to have an unusual name? What are the advantages and the disadvantages? Is it easier for girls to have unusual names than boys? Why? Is it fair? Think of some good, distinctive names for both girls and boys.

• Dream up a recipe for an unusual sandwich.

• Come up with another recipe for some other food.

• If you were in the Olympics, what event would you like to compete in? In what city would you like to have the Olympics held? What do you think that city would be like? What adventures do you think you might have while you're there?

- You're climbing Mt. Everest. Describe your adventure.

- You're on a boat going up the Amazon. Describe the ride.

- Think of good explanations for some of the things we see around us. There are no points awarded for getting a correct answer.

We're looking for creative answers here, not necessarily accurate ones. For instance:

- Why does the moon seem to grow and shrink?

- Why do the leaves fall off the trees in autumn?

- Why do wolves howl?

- Why do beavers build dams?

- Why does the sun always rise in the East and set in the West?

- Why are male birds more colorful than female birds?

- Why are some clouds white and some dark?

- Why does the wind blow?

- Why do rivers flow instead of standing still like the water in a swimming pool?

- Why do trees have rings in their trunks?

- Why do stars twinkle?

- What makes the wind blow?

- At one time astronomers didn't know about the existence of all the planets we know about now. Suppose more planets were discovered in the future. Pick a name for the next planet to be discovered.

- Some things usually make people unhappy, like a broken toy, a rainy day, or a bad report card. Can you think of anything good about these things? Think of more things that usually make people unhappy—and try to think of good things about them, too.

• Colors sometimes have fancy names, especially when they're colors of paint, crayons, or nail polish. Instead of just "black" there's "crushed black velvet." Instead of "orange" there's "juicy tangerine." Can you think of some interesting, descriptive names for any colors?

• If a visitor from outer space landed here, what would you show him or her first? What would you show this visitor as the most important things on our planet? What would most show what a great planet we live on? What would you show the visitor as examples of the bad side of life on Earth? What would you show off as the prettiest things on Earth? What else would you show him or her? What would you ask the visitor about life on his or her planet? If the visitor offered to take you on a trip back to his or her planet, would you go? Why?

• If an exchange student were visiting your town, what would you show him or her as things your town can be proud of? If you could take the student on a cross-country trip, what would you show off? Would you show him or her the less-good parts of our country? Why? What things are less than good? What can we do about changing them?

• How could your city or town be improved?

• How could your school be improved?

• What is the most important quality in a friend? How can you be a better friend? How could your friends be better friends to you and their other friends?

• In what way could you be a better person?

• How could you earn money right now if you wanted to?

• If you could have any job in the world as an adult, what would it be? Suppose it were a job that doesn't even exist now. Invent a job that may not exist but that you'd like to have when you grow up.

• If you could pass any laws, what would they be? What

effect would these laws have on your life? On the whole world? Is there a downside to passing these laws?

• If you could repeal any laws, that is, make it so they're not laws anymore, which ones would you repeal? What effect would repealing these laws have on your life? On the whole world? Is there a downside to repealing these laws?

• What is the near future going to be like? What changes will occur in the world, in technology, in the ways we live, in ten years? In twenty? In fifty?

Your child can extrapolate the look and feel of the near future from the texture of life in the present. What improvements will have been made in modern technology by them? What will computers be able to do? How about phones? Any totally new gadgets? How will such problems as pollution, warring countries, ozone depletion, overpopulation, and poverty have been solved—or will they be bigger than ever? What will the new problems be? What will kids be playing with in ten, twenty, or fifty years? What will schools be like? Will there be a single European currency? Will another planet or artificial satellite have been colonized? What kind of music will be popular?

• A simile is a comparison using the words *like* or *as* to describe something, such as "deep as a well," "dark as night," "easy as pie." Many similes are old and tired; they have been used too often. Others don't mean much to many people—for instance, the expressions "black as soot," or "black as pitch." You probably don't know what pitch is, and you may not know what soot is either. So invent some similes that are meaningful to you. Complete these similes:

• White as _____
• Black as _____
• Happy as _____

- Sad as _____
- Dreary as _____
- Hopeful as _____
- Cross as _____
- Mean as _____
- Unfair as _____
- Unreal as _____
- Red as _____
- Blue as _____
- Bright as _____
- Dull as _____
- Unbelievable as _____

Now think up some other similes.

- If you had two heads, what could you do that you can't do now?

- If you had eyes in the back of your head, what would you be able to do?

- Suppose you had four hands. What could you do that you can't do now?

- Suppose you could make yourself invisible? What would you do?

- What would you do with X-ray vision?

- If you could have three wishes come true, what would you wish for?

- Suppose you could have five wishes, but none of them could be for yourself? What would you wish for then?

- How many unusual uses can you think of for a hat? (Replies might include, "to plant flowers in," "to carry sand home from the beach," or "carry my lunch in it on a picnic so I have it to keep the sun out of my eyes." After you've exhausted the possible uses of a hat, pick another item to find unusual uses for.)

• If you could go back through your life, what one event would you change, and in what way? Why? In what ways would your life in the time since that moment be different?

• If you could change or undo anything that happened in the history of the whole world, what would it be? What would be your next two or three choices, and why?

• If you were a coin lying on the street, who would you like to be found by, and why? What would you like that person to spend you on?

• If you could be any animal in the world, what animal would you like to be? Why? What are the good things about being that animal? What are the drawbacks?

• You can spend one hundred dollars a day for a week. How would you spend the money?

• You can spend one hundred dollars a day for a week, but you may not spend any of the money on yourself. How would you spend it?

• If you were given one million dollars on your birthday every year for the rest of your life, what would you do with the money? How would your life change?

• In what ways *wouldn't* your life change even if you got a million dollars?

• You are going to spend a week on a deserted island. You can only bring one suitcase. What would you pack in it?

• You are going to spend a week on a deserted island. You may bring four books, two audio tapes, and one friend. Which books, tapes, and friend would you bring along? Explain the reasons for your choices.

• What dead inventor would you like to see come back to

life in order to see what the world is like today? Why did you pick this person?

• You have the opportunity to start a colony on another planet. What would you need to take with you? What are going to be the biggest problems facing you and your colonists? What will be the easiest thing for you and your colonists about your new lives on the planet?

• Your TV is broken. The repairman says it will take two weeks to get it fixed. You need to plan to fill the time you usually spend watching TV with other activities. What are you going to do in that time?

• Write a "recipe" for friendship.

• You're riding an exercise bike when suddenly it takes off into the sky. Where do you go? What do you see? Where does it land? Does anything interesting happen to you after it lands? How are you going to get back home?

• You're in an antiques store and find a watch engraved "Lila—I will always love you. Edward." Talk about Lila and Edward. Who were they? What is the story about them, including the time after he gave her the watch? How did the watch wind up in the antiques store?

• You are a snowflake. Describe your creation, your descent to earth, and your life once you landed on the ground.

• Name all the famous places you'd like to see and explain why you chose each one.

• Your friend is really mad at you. He won't even talk to you. The worst part is, you haven't a clue why he's upset with you. How are you going to find out what's going on?

• Your best friend doesn't invite you to her birthday party. What do you think her reason might be?

• You're a pawn in a chess game. What are your thoughts?

• You wake up one morning and find you've traded bodies

with your dog. Your brain is in your dog's body and vice versa. How would you spend your day?

• How could two people who don't speak the same language manage to communicate?

• All the electricity in the world goes out for one day. What would some of the consequences be worldwide? How would it affect you personally? What would some of the worst things be that would happen? Are there any good sides to this happening? What are they?

• If you had to give up all but one of the electrical or battery-operated appliances in your house, what one would you choose to keep? Why?

• If all the water in the world froze solid for one day, how would this affect you? How would it affect other people? What would be the best thing about it? The worst thing?

• You're at the beach. Digging along the shore, you find a sunken treasure. What is it? What do you do when you find it? Whom do you tell? What things will change in your life as a result? What's the best part? Is there any bad side to it?

• Suppose every time you opened your microwave's door you found hot food in it. What would you do with all that food?

• A really rich but really strange relative has died and left you his or her house. The house is just as strange as this relative was. Describe the house, the furniture, and other stuff in it.

• You have to take one additional class. It does not have to be a class that your real school currently offers—it can be anything. What class would you take?

• A fortune-teller tells you it's really important that you use the next year of your life in the wisest way possible. You want to follow her instructions. What sorts of things are you going to do?

• You are a newborn baby, but one who already knows everything you actually now know in real life. What would you say or do to amaze people? Whom would you most like to amaze?

• You have a full-grown adult's mind but the body of a little child. What would you do? How would you act?

• You wake up tomorrow and find you have the body of a full-grown adult, but your mind, knowledge, and way of thinking are all the same as they were when you went to bed the night before. What would you do? In what ways would your life be different?

• Your favorite piece of clothing is too small. You have to get rid of it. What are some of its memories about its life with you? What do you suppose the next part of its life will be like?

• Walking down the street, you find a feather. Where do you suppose it came from? What were some of its adventures? You pick it up and carry it down the street but accidentally drop it down a storm sewer. What are its adventures going to be now?

• You are a child's favorite stuffed toy. Describe your life.

• You are an unhappy prince or princess. You have a castle, servants, and lots of money, but you're not happy. Why? What would you need in order to be happy?

• You are a picture in a frame on a wall. Whose wall are you on, and what do you see?

• Describe the daily life of a homeless person.

• You're a teacher, and a child in your class misbehaves. What's a good way to discipline him or her?

• You swallow a magic pill that makes you invisible. What kinds of problems or adventures might you have?

• You have invented the most powerful telescope in the world. What do you see? What discoveries do you make?

• You find a piece of a treasure map. Where would you look for the rest of the map? Then what do you do?

• You are ten feet tall for one hour. How does that change

your life? What will you do that's different? How does your height affect the people around you?

• If you could be any person, living or dead, of any nationality, who would you choose to be, and why? What would be the best part about being that person? Is there a bad side to it? What is it?

• What would happen if, instead of being born little and growing, we were born completely grown up and got younger every year? How would life be different?

• If dogs ran the world, what would it be like?

• If your tennis shoes could talk, what would they say?

• If you could make a request of any one person in the world, knowing that whoever it was had to say yes, whom would you ask and what would the request be?

• What-if questions are fun, too. A what-if question supposes that either a fictional story or true history would have ended differently if events had been altered. Some what-if questions to ask your child are:

• What if Lincoln had been too tired to go to the theater that night?

• What if Practical Pig's house didn't have a fireplace?

• What if someone else's foot had been small enough to fit in Cinderella's slipper, and the Prince got to the other woman's house first?

• What if the boat had tipped over when Washington stood up in it? (Suppose he didn't drown, just got awfully wet—would that have affected history in any way?)

• What if Lee Harvey Oswald had only wounded Kennedy, and the President recovered?

• What if Wendy, Michael, and John had chosen to stay in Never-Never Land with Peter instead of flying home again? And what if the crocodile's clock hadn't run down, and it wasn't able to sneak up on Hook?

If your child isn't familiar with some of the stories or history in the examples above, feel free to substitute other what-if questions. And even if your child does know all those references, you can still think of more questions to throw at him or her.

• What-if questions don't have to be proposed all bunched together in a special session; when you've just finished reading a book to your child or telling her a slice of history, that's a good time to add, "Now suppose things had been different? What if we'd been able to win World War II without dropping The Bomb?" (That's a what-if for an older child.)

You can even apply what-if questions to family history: "What if Grandma hadn't lost the Miss Wyoming contest? What if she'd been elected Miss America?"

Creativity—it's important no matter what your aspirations for your child are, no matter what his interests or eventual career choice may be. Creativity helps the plumber who's up against a seemingly insurmountable piping problem as well as it helps the sculptor or playwright. It helps the woman—or man—cooking the family's nightly dinner, as well as the chef devising a new recipe or perfecting a sumptuous banquet and making it visually appealing.

It helps the architect designing a skyscraper or a suburban home, the lawyer crafting a closing statement to the jury, and the teacher finding a new way to make lessons come alive for his or her students. It helps the parent dealing with the realities of child-raising. Haven't you searched for a creative solution to a problem with your child, or a creative punishment that will correct your child's behavior or attitude in a fair and meaningful way?

Creativity enriches our lives in many ways—our personal lives as well as our professional lives, and the latter whether we are poets or plumbers. Or kids applying creativity to homework, play, or problem-solving.

Give your child a good head start. Raise a creative child. Start today: It's never too late...or too early.

Index